Loving Someone with Endometriosis

A Partner's Compassionate Guide to Chronic Pelvic Pain, Invisible Flares, and Building an Intimate Life Beyond the Diagnosis

Hannah Georgina Wright

This book is intended for general informational and educational purposes only. The content does not constitute medical, clinical, psychological, or professional advice of any kind. Nothing in this book is a substitute for consultation with a qualified healthcare professional regarding any medical condition, treatment, or health concern. The author and publisher make no representations or warranties regarding the accuracy, completeness, or fitness of the information for any particular purpose and accept no liability for any outcomes arising from the use or application of the material presented here.

The names, characters, scenarios, and illustrative examples used throughout this book are composite constructions created for educational purposes. Any resemblance to specific individuals, living or deceased, is coincidental and unintentional. Nothing in this book is intended to harm, misrepresent, or defame any person or entity.

Readers are encouraged to apply the information in this book in ways that are appropriate to their own circumstances and with the support of qualified professionals where needed. The publisher and author specifically disclaim any and all liability, loss, or risk incurred as a consequence, directly or indirectly, of the use and application of any of the contents of this book.

First Edition:2026

ISBN: 978-1-7647265-5-9

Table of Contents

Preface

The research literature on endometriosis has expanded substantially over the past two decades. Clinical understanding of the disease, including its mechanisms, its surgical management, and its documented consequences for physical health, psychological wellbeing, fertility, and quality of life, has advanced considerably from the position of a generation ago. What the literature has not kept pace with is the experience of the people who live alongside the estimated 190 million affected globally. Partners, spouses, and family caregivers of people with endometriosis occupy a specific and largely unaddressed position in both clinical settings and in the available self-help landscape.

This book is a partner-facing guide to endometriosis, which is to say it is not a patient guide adapted for adjacent readers. It was designed from its structure outward for people who are not experiencing the condition themselves but whose relational, practical, and emotional lives are shaped by it daily. Endometriosis is a systemic inflammatory disease in which tissue similar to the uterine lining grows outside the uterus, causing cyclic inflammation, adhesions, and pain that does not resolve without clinical intervention. Understanding this biology, the mechanisms by which it produces pain, the surgical approaches used to address it, and the systemic factors that have delayed diagnosis for a generation of patients, forms the clinical foundation on which everything else in this book is built.

The central problem this book addresses is not a shortage of empathy among supporting partners. Those who seek a structured guide to this subject are, in most cases, already trying to help. The gap is structural. Without understanding what endometriosis does in the body, why pain does not reliably track with visible disease extent, what distinguishes excision surgery from ablation, or why pelvic floor physiotherapy addresses a dimension of the condition that surgery alone does not resolve, a partner's capacity to be useful is constrained by information rather than intention. This book provides that information in accessible terms, organized around the specific situations partners actually face.

The framework applied throughout is sequential and practical. Each chapter addresses a defined domain of the partner's experience, from clinical understanding and flare management through surgical support, healthcare advocacy, intimacy, fertility, emotional processing, and the sustained demands of a long-term chronic illness partnership. Chapters close with targeted action steps rooted in each chapter's core principle and grounded in the research literature. The composite cases used throughout are drawn from documented patterns in the published literature on endometriosis partnerships and constructed with appropriate care for privacy and accuracy.

This is not a memoir, and it does not rest its authority on personal testimony. Its primary readers are partners and spouses of people diagnosed with, or awaiting assessment for, endometriosis. The frameworks presented will also be of use to parents, close family members, and anyone providing sustained support to someone living with this condition.

This book will not resolve endometriosis, and it does not promise any specific clinical, relational, or fertility outcome. What it offers is more bounded and more practical: a structured resource for caregiving partners who want the clinical literacy, the communication tools, and the emotional framework to be genuinely present and genuinely capable in one of the more demanding relational situations a partnership can face.

Introduction: The Other Side of the Diagnosis

The hospital corridor outside consultation room four was beige and quiet and smelled like hand sanitizer. Oscar had been sitting on one of the plastic chairs for forty minutes, watching the light change under the door.

He'd brought a book. He hadn't opened it. He'd been telling himself this appointment was different. That they'd found something. That the consultant had actually looked at the scans properly. That after three years of "we can't find anything" and "perhaps keep a pain diary" and "many women experience some discomfort with their cycles," this was the visit where somebody finally said a thing that made sense.

The door opened. Eloise walked out.

He stood up too fast and knocked his takeaway coffee off the arm of the chair. He didn't pick it up. He was watching her face.

She'd been crying. Her mascara had run in the way it did when she pressed her fingers under her eyes, which she did when she was trying not to cry in front of strangers. She was holding a folded printout.

He asked if she was okay. She said she was fine. He asked what they'd said. She handed him the printout without speaking.

Stage 3 endometriosis. Extensive pelvic adhesions. Bilateral ovarian involvement. Surgical management recommended.

He stood in that corridor reading the same sentence three times. He was a practical man. He dealt with problems. He had once talked Eloise through a presentation she was certain she was going to fail, sentence by sentence in a car park at seven in the morning, until she walked in and delivered it. He was good in a crisis.

He stood in that corridor with a printout in his hand and a spreading pool of cold coffee near his left foot, and he had absolutely nothing.

That is the moment this book is for.

Not the diagnosis, or the surgery to come, or the seven years that had led to that corridor. The moment when someone you love has just been told something significant and you want very much to help and you have no idea how.

This Book Is for You

This book is for you. Not for her. There are hundreds of books for her. Patient memoirs, dietary guides, surgical explainers, symptom journals, online communities with hundreds of thousands of members. An entire ecosystem of support built, slowly and imperfectly, for the person who has endometriosis. What hasn't been built is the guide for the person sitting in the corridor outside.

The partner who is confused. The partner who is helpless. The partner who has stood in doorways not knowing whether to knock and who has said the wrong thing, and said nothing, and said something well-intentioned that landed terribly, and who keeps trying anyway because the person they love is in pain and they cannot stand that they can't fix it.

That's the principle this book runs on: understanding doesn't cure endometriosis, but it changes everything about how you live alongside it. The partner who understands what a flare involves can respond to one with calm instead of panic. The partner who understands the surgical options can ask an intelligent question at the consultation instead of sitting silent. The partner who has language for the fertility grief can say something real instead of reaching for a platitude that lands in the wrong place.

Understanding is the first tool. Everything else in this book builds on it.

The Shape of This Experience

You might be a partner of three months or fifteen years. You might have watched the same crisis play out in different bedrooms and waiting rooms, each time feeling less equipped than the last. You might be a parent, holding steady for a daughter in her twenties who keeps being sent home without answers. You might be new to all of this, a few months into a relationship where someone you're falling for has shared a folder of appointment notes and said, quietly: there's something you should know about me.

Whoever you are, this experience tends to move through the same stages.

First comes confusion. What is this exactly. Why does it cause this much pain. Why did it take so long to get a name for it. Why do some days seem fine and others seem impossible. You want to understand, and the medical system isn't designed to help you understand. It's designed to treat her, and only her, and only sometimes.

Then comes helplessness. She's in pain and nothing you do seems to make a real difference. You say the wrong thing. You do the wrong thing. Sometimes you do nothing because nothing feels safer than something, and it still isn't right.

Then comes something quieter and harder. Guilt, because you've felt frustrated about cancelled plans and then felt terrible for it. Loneliness, because you can't talk about this the way she can. And a particular kind of grief: not grief for her, which you know how to name, but grief for the version of your life together you'd imagined, which is going to look different from what you pictured, and you're not sure yet what that looks like.

Nobody asks about these stages. Nobody offers a guide for where you're standing.

That changes now.

There's a version of this experience that most partners share. It goes roughly like this. In the early months, you're still learning the shape of it: the bad weeks, the cancelled plans, the clinical appointments that produce nothing, the dawning understanding that this isn't temporary. Then comes a longer middle period, measured in years for many couples, in which you adapt. The adaptation is real. You get better at the flares. You learn what to say and what not to say. You develop a kind of operational competence.

But beneath that competence, the things you haven't processed accumulate. The loneliness is still there. The grief about fertility, if that's a dimension of your situation, tends to arrive later than everything else, and when it does it often arrives with force. The resentment and the guilt about the resentment, which is its own kind of exhausting loop, persists. And there's a particular fatigue that belongs to the partner specifically: the fatigue of being the stable one, the one who holds things, for months and years and without a designated space to set it down.

This book tries to give you that space. Not to burden it with everything that's been left unprocessed. But to open it up a little.

That version of the buffer day story matters because it illustrates something about the endometriosis partnership that doesn't get said enough: so much of the competence that a partner develops is invisible. It develops in the margins. It takes years and it isn't acknowledged, because there's no framework in which it's acknowledged, and there's no community where partners debrief what they've learned.

That's another thing this book is trying to change. The partner of someone with endometriosis has a real body of experience. The management strategies, the pre-flare reading, the appointment preparation, the conversation scripts that work and the ones that don't: these are real skills that real people develop. This book tries to compress that learning curve. You don't have to wait two years to build Mateo's buffer day habit. You can build it now, because someone else already figured out that it works.

What This Book Will Do

Over the chapters ahead, you'll learn what endometriosis actually is and why it took so long to get a diagnosis. You'll learn what happens in her body during a flare and exactly what to do about it. You'll learn the difference between the two main surgical approaches, what post-operative care involves, and what your specific role looks like before and after surgery. You'll learn how to walk into a clinic as a participant rather than a spectator. You'll find room to work through the fertility conversation, the intimacy conversation, and the conversations you've been putting off because you couldn't find the right words.

You'll also find room to process what this experience is doing to you. Not just to her. To you.

Your guilt is real. Your loneliness is real. Your grief is real. Those don't make you a bad partner. They make you a person navigating something genuinely hard without a map. This book is the map. It's incomplete, because every relationship is different. But it's the first one written for where you're standing.

What This Book Won't Do

This book isn't a substitute for medical care. It doesn't replace clinical judgment from a healthcare provider who knows your situation. Where it offers scripts, they're starting points, not lines to read verbatim. Where it offers clinical explanations, they're orientations to help you understand the landscape, not diagnoses to act on alone.

It also won't promise that everything will be fine. Some of this is hard and stays hard. A chapter on intimacy can't eliminate dyspareunia. A flare protocol can't stop flares. What it can do is give you better tools for navigating something most couples navigate entirely blind.

A Brief Orientation

If you're entirely new to endometriosis, here's enough to begin. Chapter 1 goes much deeper.

Endometriosis is a condition where tissue similar to the lining of the uterus grows outside the uterus, most commonly on the ovaries, fallopian tubes, the lining of the pelvic cavity, and the bowel. This tissue responds to the same hormonal signals as the uterine lining: it thickens, breaks down, and bleeds with each menstrual cycle. Unlike the uterine lining, it has nowhere to go. It causes inflammation, scar tissue, and adhesions.

The result is pain. Often severe, recurring, cycle-related pain. Chronic pelvic pain. Painful periods. Pain during or after sex. Pain with bowel movements. Fatigue that doesn't respond to sleep.

Endometriosis isn't rare. The World Health Organization estimates it affects approximately 190 million reproductive-age women and girls globally (WHO, 2025). It isn't caused by anything you or she did. It isn't, despite what multiple doctors may have suggested, normal period pain. And despite being one of the most common gynecological conditions in the world, published reviews continue to report long diagnostic delays, with average delays around 6.6 to 6.8 years across international studies (Fryer et al., 2025). In the United Kingdom, a 2024 survey reported an average delay of 8 years and 10 months (Endometriosis UK, 2024).

Here is something the orientation needs to include, because partners consistently say nobody told them this: endometriosis is not a condition that gets diagnosed and resolved. It's managed. There are treatments that reduce symptoms, there are surgical approaches that remove visible disease, and there are hormonal therapies that suppress the cycle that drives it. But there isn't a cure in the conventional sense. What that means for you is that you're not preparing for a crisis with an endpoint. You're preparing for a different kind of long-term partnership, one in which medical management is an ongoing feature of her life and, by extension, of yours.

That isn't a reason to be frightened. It's a reason to be equipped. The couples who navigate this best aren't the ones who fight hardest against the condition. They're the ones who've learned to live intelligently alongside it. This book is about how to become one of those couples.

Chapter 1 is where that story starts.

How to Use This Book

Read it in order once if you can. The chapters are built to scaffold, moving from clinical understanding through practical crisis management to the relational and emotional dimensions of a long-term endometriosis partnership. After that first read, use it as a reference. Chapter 4 is the one to reach for when she's in a flare. Chapter 6 is the one to read before an appointment. Chapter 7 is where you start when the intimacy conversation feels necessary but impossible.

Some chapters will feel more urgent depending on where you are in the story. If surgery is coming soon, Chapter 5 is the one to read this week. If you've just received the diagnosis and she's in the early stages of grief, the Introduction and Chapter 1 will do the most immediate work. If you've been navigating this for years and the relationship is showing the strain, Chapter 8 is the one to turn to.

You don't have to read it alone. Some couples find it useful to read chapters together, particularly the ones on intimacy and fertility. Others find it more useful to read separately and then talk. There's no rule. The only rule is that you're reading it at all, which means you've decided to be more equipped, and that tends to matter more than the method.

One last practical note: the action steps in this book are placed mid-chapter, not just at the end. That's deliberate. The research on behavior change is consistent that people are most likely to act on an insight in the moment of recognition, not after more explanation. When an action step appears, it means something just became clear enough to act on. That's the right moment.

This book uses "she" for the person with endometriosis throughout. Endometriosis primarily affects people with female reproductive anatomy, and the research it draws on largely studied female patients. If "she" isn't the right word for your situation, adjust as needed. The experience it describes belongs to every partner who has stood in the corridor not knowing what to say.

> **Action Step:** Action Step: Before you go further, do this tonight. Write down, in one paragraph, what the hardest part of this experience has been so far. Not the hardest part for her. The hardest part for you. Be specific and honest. Nobody else will read this unless you choose to show them. If it's not knowing what to do during a flare, write that. If it's the fear about fertility, write that. If it's the loneliness, the guilt, the grief, write that. Keep it. You'll return to it at the end of this book, and you'll want to see what has shifted.

In Summary

The partner's experience with endometriosis is real, specific, and almost entirely without resources until now. This book is built on one principle: understanding changes what you can do and who you can be in this situation. The partner who understands the disease, the medical system, and the emotional landscape responds better, communicates better, and stays whole alongside someone they love. Nothing in these pages requires a medical background. Everything draws on peer-reviewed research and the documented experience of thousands of couples who have navigated exactly this. You didn't choose this situation. You chose to be better prepared for it, which is a different and more important thing entirely. Oscar stood in that corridor with nothing. That corridor is where this book begins. You're already past it.

Chapter 1: The Disease That Waited Seven Years to Have a Name

Martin had accompanied Clara to fourteen medical appointments before the fifteenth one changed things.

He kept count because Clara kept a spreadsheet. She was methodical like that, even about her own suffering. She'd entered each appointment with a date, a clinician name, a summary of what had been said, and a column she'd labelled "taken seriously (Y/N)." Martin had watched the N column fill up over two years. GP visits, urgent care attendances, a referral to gastroenterology that led nowhere, two separate reassurances from two separate gynaecologists that her pelvic pain was probably cycle-related and would likely settle.

The fifteenth appointment was at a specialist endometriosis clinic Clara had found after three months of research. She'd drafted a referral request letter, submitted it twice, and asked Martin to take the day off work to come with her because, she said, she didn't trust herself not to back down if they tried to dismiss her again.

They sat in the waiting room together for over an hour. Martin brought two coffees and watched Clara hold hers without drinking it. She was doing the thing she did before appointments: sitting very still, preparing herself to fight.

The consultant was a woman in her fifties with precise, attentive eyes. She read Clara's history in full. She asked specific, detailed questions. She said, partway through the consultation: I think we need to get you into surgery. I suspect we're looking at at least Stage 2. It could be more.

Clara said: so it's real.

The consultant said: yes. It's real.

Martin looked at Clara's face when she heard that. He had been in fourteen appointment rooms with her. He'd watched her be told that many women experience this, that painful periods were normal, that perhaps a food diary might help identify triggers. He'd watched her walk out of those rooms pressing her fingers under her eyes. Now he watched her receive confirmation of something she'd known for years, from a system that had taken years to confirm it, and he couldn't name, exactly, what he felt.

Something between relief and fury. And below that, something he hadn't let himself acknowledge properly until that moment: guilt. For every time he'd privately wondered whether she was catastrophizing. For every time he'd thought, half-consciously, maybe it really will get better on its own.

The principle of this chapter is simple. The diagnostic delay in endometriosis isn't a medical mystery. It's a documented, systemic failure with known and recurring causes. Understanding why it happened is the first step toward not being blindsided by what comes next, whether that means a late diagnosis, a contested one, or a treatment path that doesn't start where it should.

What Endometriosis Actually Is

The word itself tells you almost nothing about what the condition does in the body. Start here.

The uterus is lined with tissue called the endometrium. During a typical menstrual cycle, this lining thickens in preparation for a possible pregnancy. When pregnancy doesn't occur, the lining breaks down and leaves the body. In endometriosis, tissue similar to the endometrium grows outside the uterus. It can appear on the ovaries, the fallopian tubes, the outer surface of the uterus, the lining of the pelvic cavity, the bowel, the bladder, and in more severe presentations, further afield.

This tissue responds to the same hormonal signals as the uterine lining. It thickens, breaks down, and bleeds with each cycle. But unlike the uterine lining, it has nowhere to go. It bleeds into the surrounding tissue, causing inflammation, scar tissue, and adhesions. Adhesions are bands of scar tissue that cause structures to stick together: an ovary adhered to the pelvic wall, the bowel adhered to the uterus. These adhesions distort anatomy, restrict movement, and cause pain. Chronic pelvic pain. Painful periods, often severe. Dyspareunia, which is pain during or after sex. Pain with bowel movements, with urination, with physical exertion. A fatigue that isn't proportional to how much she's been doing.

The condition is estrogen-dependent: the lesions grow in response to estrogen. This is why most hormonal treatments work by suppressing it, which carries its own costs, and why symptoms often reduce after menopause. It's also why adolescents, whose estrogen levels are rising, can develop significant endometriosis during the years when pelvic pain is most likely to be dismissed as normal growing pains.

> **Teaching Point:** *Endometriosis is not normal period pain. It is a systemic inflammatory disease that causes documented, measurable, progressive damage. Characterizing it as routine discomfort isn't just unhelpful. It's wrong.*

The ASRM Stages and Why They Can Mislead

You may encounter a staging system. The American Society for Reproductive Medicine classifies endometriosis in four stages based on the extent and location of lesions and the severity of adhesions.

Stage 1 is minimal. Stage 2 is mild. Stage 3 is moderate. Stage 4 is severe.

These stages are clinically useful for guiding surgical and fertility treatment decisions. They're not useful for predicting pain. A woman with Stage 1 endometriosis can be in debilitating pain. A woman with Stage 4 can have moderate symptoms. The staging reflects the visible extent of the disease at surgery, not its functional impact on the person living with it.

What this means practically: don't calibrate your understanding of how serious things are to the number on the surgical report. Clara's Stage 2 diagnosis meant nothing about whether her pain was reasonable or disproportionate. Martin had spent two years, privately and guiltily, wondering whether she was making too much of it. The stage confirmed the disease's existence. It said nothing about the validity of the years before it.

It also said nothing about how well she'd function in the weeks after surgery. Stage is a snapshot of visible disease at one moment in time. It doesn't capture nerve sensitization, the psychological weight of years of dismissal, or the degree to which her body has adapted its pain signaling over time. Two women with identical ASRM staging can have completely different daily experiences. The number is a starting point for clinical conversation, not a verdict on how much her pain matters.

> **Action Step:** Observation Challenge: In your next conversation with her about her health, notice what you assume before she's finished speaking. Do you find yourself calibrating how seriously to take what she's saying based on a previous medical opinion, a good day she's had recently, or the fact that she looks well right now? Write down the assumption. Don't act on it. Just see it.

The Seven-Year Question

There's a number that tends to stop people the first time they encounter it. The average time between a person experiencing first symptoms of endometriosis and receiving a confirmed diagnosis is commonly reported at about 6.6 to 6.8 years across international studies, with wide variation by country and study design (Fryer et al., 2025).

Some studies included in that review reported average delays of just over 11 years in the United States. In the United Kingdom, a 2024 survey of 4,371 diagnosed women found the average delay had risen to 8 years and 10 months, an increase of 10 months since 2020 (Endometriosis UK, 2024). The same survey found that 78% of women had been told by at least one clinician that they were 'making a fuss about nothing' or words to that effect (Endometriosis UK, 2024).

Think about what that means. The average woman with endometriosis spends between seven and eleven years in pain, seeking help, and being sent home. She may have tried four, six, eight different clinicians. She's probably been told her symptoms are normal at least once, likely many times. She's developed, in that time, a sophisticated wariness about whether the medical system will help her. A habit of minimizing, not because she wants to, but because describing pain accurately has so often led to dismissal that self-minimizing feels safer.

By the time she sits across from a consultant who finally says yes, I think this is what it is, she's been carrying this alone for the better part of a decade. The relief in that moment is real. So is the grief. All those years. All those appointments. All those times she was right and was told she wasn't.

Martin had been with Clara for two of her seven years. For the five years before they met, she'd been navigating it alone.

Why the System Keeps Missing It

The delay isn't random. Its causes are documented and recurring across healthcare systems and countries.

The first is the normalization of period pain. Menstrual pain is culturally understood as expected. "Painful periods" isn't a red-flag phrase in most primary care consultation models. When a woman presents with severe cyclical pelvic pain, the first-line response in many systems is to manage the pain, not to investigate its cause. Analgesics. Hormonal contraceptives. A pain diary.

The second is a diagnostic limitation. Endometriosis can't be reliably identified through a standard pelvic ultrasound unless it presents as an ovarian cyst, called an endometrioma. Superficial peritoneal lesions, deep infiltrating lesions, and many adhesions are invisible on standard ultrasound. They can be missed on MRI. The only way to definitively diagnose endometriosis is through laparoscopy, which is a surgical procedure. Healthcare systems are understandably reluctant to move to surgery without exhausting other investigative steps, which adds time.

The third is a training gap. Endometriosis education in medical training has historically been inadequate. Many general practitioners have limited confidence in recognizing the symptom pattern. Many gynaecologists haven't trained in specialist endometriosis surgery. NICE updated its guidance in 2024, but the implementation of guidance takes time to filter through a system (NICE, 2024).

The fourth, and the hardest to quantify, is a credibility problem. The research literature documents a consistent pattern in which women's self-reported pain is systematically discounted in clinical settings. The 78% dismissal figure is a data point. Behind it are millions of individual consultations where a woman described her pain accurately and was told, implicitly or explicitly, that it couldn't be as serious as she was suggesting.

Clara had known for years. She'd kept the spreadsheet because she needed documentation of a pattern she was afraid a new clinician would dismiss as anecdote.

What Those Years Actually Cost

The delay isn't only a matter of suffering accumulated over time. It has measurable clinical consequences.

Endometriosis is a progressive condition in many cases. Without treatment, adhesions can develop and spread. Ovarian involvement can reduce ovarian reserve, affecting fertility.

Lesions on the bowel or bladder can cause organ damage that requires more complex surgical intervention than earlier-stage disease would have needed. The cost of waiting isn't neutral.

The psychological costs are equally documented. Women with endometriosis report substantial social and psychological effects, including anxiety, depression, reduced quality of life, and effects from delayed recognition and dismissal (Culley et al., 2013). They develop anticipatory patterns: dreading the cycle, dreading sex, dreading appointments. This anticipatory layer means the psychological cost of endometriosis doesn't only happen during flares. It happens in the spaces between them.

There's a quality to long-delayed diagnoses that's different from early ones. The woman who is diagnosed after seven years has also spent seven years developing her coping infrastructure. She's learned which colleagues she can tell and which she can't. She's learned how to manage the worst days in ways that are invisible to most people around her. She's learned to hold the experience of significant pain somewhat separately from her social self, because integrating it would be too costly.

This means that by the time she has a name for what she's been living with, she has also been carrying it alone for a very long time. The diagnosis doesn't automatically redistribute that weight. It often takes a deliberate effort, from her and from the people who love her, to let it be more shared than it has been.

Partners carry something across those years too. Martin had felt guilty for every moment of private skepticism. He'd felt furious at every dismissal. He'd felt, more than once, that he was failing her by not finding a way through a system that didn't want to be found. He wasn't. But there's no one to tell you that when you're in it.

> **Action Step:** Writing Challenge: Find out, or recall if you already know: when did she first experience symptoms that might have been endometriosis? When was she diagnosed? Calculate the gap between those two dates. Write it down. Then write one sentence about what you know she went through in those years, and one sentence about what you went through alongside her. Not to fix it. Just to see it clearly.

The Anger Is Appropriate

Something worth saying plainly: if you're angry, you're right to be.

The anger at a medical system that took seven, eight, ten years to confirm what the person you love had been telling it for years is a reasonable response to a documented injustice. It doesn't need to be managed into something more palatable. It needs to be named.

What to do with it is a more practical question. Some of it goes into becoming a better advocate in clinical settings, which Chapter 6 addresses directly. Some of it goes into understanding the disease well enough to have conversations that clinicians take seriously. Some of it, with time, goes toward releasing her from the suspicion that she might have been wrong about what she knew. She wasn't. She waited a very long time to be believed.

> **Teaching Point:** *The 78% of women who reported being told they were making a fuss aren't outliers. They're the majority.*

> *The dismissal wasn't a failure of individual clinicians. It's a documented pattern in how women's pain has been received inside medical systems across countries and decades.*

In Summary

Endometriosis is a systemic inflammatory condition where tissue similar to the uterine lining grows outside the uterus, causing inflammation, adhesions, and progressive damage. It affects approximately 190 million people globally and has an average diagnostic delay of 6.6 years, rising to nearly 9 years in the UK and over 11 in the US. The delay has documented causes: the normalization of menstrual pain, the limitations of non-surgical diagnostics, inadequate clinical training, and a systemic pattern of discounting women's self-reported pain. The staging system doesn't predict pain severity, which means a Stage 1 diagnosis doesn't mean a mild experience. The anger about those years is appropriate. Understanding why they happened is where preparation begins. Martin's guilt about his private skepticism was understandable. The system that produced it was not. You've done better than the system by reading this far.

Chapter 2: What Endometriosis Actually Costs -- Mapping the Full Impact

Hugo was at a dinner party when he realized he couldn't remember the last spontaneous night out they'd had.

It wasn't a dramatic realization. It came sideways, the way these things do. Someone asked what he and Noemi had been up to, and he opened his mouth and waited for something to come out, and what came out was a story about a weekend trip they'd taken eight months ago. Not because it was recent, but because it was the most vivid thing he could find.

He finished the story. He smiled. He drank some wine. On the drive home he was quiet.

Noemi asked if he was okay. He said he was fine. She asked if something had happened at the dinner. He said no, everything was fine, how was she feeling. She said tired but okay. He said good.

He didn't tell her what he'd been thinking in the car because he wasn't sure he had words for it yet. It wasn't a complaint. It was closer to a kind of mourning for a version of their life that had been quietly replaced by something else, something that was still their life but arranged differently, organized now around the calendar of her pain and the management of it, and he'd stopped noticing when that had happened.

The principle of this chapter is this: endometriosis doesn't stay in one room. It moves through every area of a shared life, the physical, the psychological, the relational, the financial, and the social. Understanding the full reach of it isn't meant to frighten. It's meant to prepare. What you can see, you can plan for.

The Physical Reach

Begin with the body, because the body is where everything else starts.

Chronic pelvic pain is the central feature of endometriosis for most diagnosed women, though its character varies significantly. For some women it's constant, a persistent background ache that spikes with certain triggers. For others it's intensely cyclic, peaking around menstruation and then receding, only to return. For some, it's both.

Dysmenorrhea, which is painful menstruation, is present in the majority of cases and is often what first drove the woman you love into clinical settings years ago. The pain during periods in endometriosis is often distinguished from typical menstrual discomfort by its severity, its resistance to standard over-the-counter analgesics, and its tendency to radiate into the lower back, the legs, and the abdomen in ways that go well beyond what most people experience as period pain.

Dyspareunia, pain during or after sex, is a common symptom of endometriosis and is frequently reported in clinical and patient-facing literature (NICE, 2024; WHO, 2025). This is one of the most practically consequential features of the condition for couples and one of the hardest to discuss. It's addressed in full in Chapter 7.

Bowel and bladder symptoms are common but often underreported, partly because they can seem unrelated to the gynecological diagnosis. Painful bowel movements, bloating, alternating constipation and diarrhea, and urinary frequency or urgency can all be features of endometriosis involving the bowel or bladder. Many women are investigated for IBS, interstitial cystitis, or irritable bowel before endometriosis is considered.

Fatigue. This is the symptom that tends to be most invisible to people outside the relationship. Endometriosis-associated fatigue is different from tiredness. It isn't resolved by a good night's sleep. It's a systemic fatigue that researchers associate with the chronic inflammatory state the condition maintains in the body (Zondervan et al., 2020). Hugo had noticed that Noemi needed more rest than she used to. He'd attributed it to work stress. It was her body working against itself.

The Psychological Reach

The psychological impact of endometriosis is documented and significant, and it operates across multiple levels.

At the level of mood and mental health, women with endometriosis report higher rates of anxiety and depression than the general population, even after controlling for the confounding effects of pain (Zarbo et al., 2018). This isn't simply because living in pain is depressing, though it is. The research suggests a more complex relationship between the inflammatory processes of the condition, the hormonal fluctuations that drive it, and the neurological systems that regulate mood.

At the level of anticipatory experience, many women develop what clinicians describe as anticipatory anxiety: a dread of the pain before it arrives, which can be almost as disabling as the pain itself. She may begin dreading sex days before she expects it to be painful. She may begin dreading her period two weeks before it starts. This anticipatory layer means the psychological cost of endometriosis doesn't only happen during flares. It happens in the spaces between them.

At the level of identity, years of dismissal by medical systems, and sometimes by the people around her, can create a particular kind of internal damage. When you spend years being told that your pain isn't as serious as you think it is, you learn to doubt your own experience. This self-doubt tends to persist even after diagnosis. You may notice it in the way she qualifies her pain. In the way she apologizes for it. In the way she sometimes seems uncertain whether she's allowed to be as bad as she actually is.

> **Teaching Point:** *When the person you love minimizes her pain to you, it isn't modesty. It's a pattern trained into her by years of medical encounters that rewarded minimizing. Understanding this changes how you hear what she says about how she's doing.*

The Relational Reach

A 2024 multicenter study involving 381 women with surgically or histologically confirmed endometriosis, 381 control women, and male partners found that chronic pain, dyspareunia, sexual dissatisfaction, fatigue, and infertility were associated with partnership strain and lower relationship happiness (el Hadad et al., 2024). Women with endometriosis reported separation thoughts more often than control women, and sexual satisfaction was strongly associated with those thoughts. Higher pain intensity in women was associated with lower partnership happiness in their male partners.

What this research confirms, in numbers, is what Hugo and Noemi had been living. The condition doesn't just affect her. It affects the relationship. It changes what's possible on any given day. It reshapes shared plans. It shifts the dynamic between two people in ways that are gradual enough to miss until, at a dinner party, someone asks what you've been up to and you realize the answer is: managing. Mostly managing.

Hugo had watched Noemi at a work event eight months after her diagnosis. She'd spent three hours being professionally competent and socially engaged. On the drive home she'd fallen asleep in the passenger seat within ten minutes. He'd watched her sleep and thought: nobody in that room knew. Nobody had any idea what she manages every day. He'd felt something complex. Proud of her, and genuinely sad for her, and a kind of loneliness that was difficult to name because it was about being the only witness to a life that looked different from the inside than it did from the outside.

That loneliness is a real feature of this experience. You know things about her daily reality that nobody else knows. You hold information about how bad certain days are that she doesn't share more widely. You carry a version of her experience that's invisible to her colleagues, her family, and often even to her friends. This is a form of intimacy, but it's also a form of isolation, and it's worth naming as such.

This isn't a reason to despair. It's a reason to name what's changed, which is what this book is trying to help you do.

> **Action Step:** Conversation Challenge: This week, ask Noemi, or the person you love, one specific question about how her experience of the condition has changed in the last six months. Not "how are you feeling" but something more particular: has the fatigue been different recently? Has she noticed any new patterns in what triggers the pain? This kind of specific, informed question communicates something important to her. It says: I've been paying attention.

The Career and Financial Reach

The economic burden of endometriosis is substantial and remarkably understudied. What research does exist paints a consistent picture.

Women with endometriosis report significant reductions in work capacity, particularly in the days surrounding menstruation and during flares. A study documenting the economic impact of the condition in Cyprus found that medical costs and productivity losses both correlated positively with the severity of pain symptoms (Matalliotakis et al., 2021). This isn't a finding about a specific country. It's a pattern documented across healthcare systems and income levels.

For couples, the financial dimensions of endometriosis can accumulate in ways that are hard to see individually but significant in aggregate. Repeated specialist consultations, often out of pocket. Prescription costs. Physical therapy and pain management. Time taken off work, sometimes by both partners. And, where fertility is affected, the costs of assisted reproductive technology, which in many countries are partially or entirely unsubsidized.

Noemi had reduced her consulting work by thirty percent in the year before her diagnosis. Hugo had covered the shortfall without discussing it directly, because discussing it felt like making her condition about money, which felt wrong. But not discussing it meant the financial stress accumulated silently between them, with no shared framework for addressing it.

Naming the financial dimension isn't callous. It's part of understanding the full picture of what you're navigating together.

Some couples find it useful to create a shared medical budget, a simple tracking document that makes the ongoing costs visible rather than letting them accumulate as unexamined stress. This doesn't mean treating the condition as a financial problem. It means removing one layer of hidden pressure from a relationship that already carries significant weight. Money stress and health stress compound each other. Separating them out, even partially, makes both more manageable.

The Invisibility Problem

There's a particular cruelty to endometriosis that distinguishes it from conditions with visible markers. It produces no outward signs. On a good day, or even on a bad one, the person who has it may look entirely well. This invisibility creates a secondary burden that operates in social and professional settings.

Hugo had watched Noemi be asked, more than once, why she was cancelling plans again. He'd watched her try to explain to colleagues why she needed to work from home on certain days. He'd heard his mother suggest that she seemed better than she had the previous year, as if better was the same as well. Each of these interactions required Noemi to explain herself to someone who had no visible evidence to work with, and who had a culturally embedded skepticism about the seriousness of menstrual pain.

The 78% dismissal figure isn't only about doctors. It's about a wider cultural pattern that endometriosis patients navigate daily, in their workplaces, their families, and their social circles. As her partner, you'll encounter this too. You'll be asked to defend, explain, or justify her condition to people who haven't seen what you've seen. Chapter 11 provides language for those situations.

One thing worth preparing for: you'll also encounter it internally. There will be days when she looks well and you'll find yourself wondering, for a moment, whether today is a day you could make plans. Then she'll tell you her cycle is starting in two days and you'll see the familiar shift in her. The "she looks fine" error is one that partners make too, not from cruelty but from the human tendency to calibrate what we expect based on what we can see. The biology of invisible illness doesn't give you visible cues. You have to develop a different kind of attention, and she has to learn that asking for it is okay.

Comorbidities and Overlapping Conditions

Endometriosis frequently co-presents with other conditions, and understanding them prevents misattribution. If her bowel symptoms worsen at a different phase of her cycle than her pelvic pain, that's useful information. If her pain with sex has a different character from her cyclical pain, that too is worth noting.

Adenomyosis is a condition in which tissue similar to the uterine lining grows within the muscle wall of the uterus itself.

It's distinct from endometriosis but frequently occurs alongside it. It causes heavy periods, severe cramping, and an enlarged, tender uterus. It's diagnosed through ultrasound or MRI and is only definitively resolved with hysterectomy.

Interstitial cystitis is a chronic bladder condition causing pelvic pain, urinary urgency, and frequency. It's diagnosed and treated separately from endometriosis but is found more commonly in endometriosis patients than in the general population.

Pelvic floor dysfunction is perhaps the most practically relevant comorbidity for partners to understand. The pelvic floor muscles can become hypertonic, which means chronically contracted and tender, in response to years of pelvic pain. This hypertonicity contributes to dyspareunia, to bowel and bladder symptoms, and to a cycle of pain that persists even when the underlying endometriosis is managed. Pelvic floor physiotherapy, addressed in Chapter 7, is among the most evidence-based treatments for this dimension of the condition.

Knowing these terms before you're in the room changes what the room is like. When a consultant mentions adenomyosis in passing and you know what it is, you can follow the conversation rather than falling behind it. When a GP recommends transvaginal ultrasound, you can ask the relevant question: what won't that ultrasound show? A partner who asks that question has read something. The clinician knows it. The conversation changes.

In Summary

Endometriosis reaches into every dimension of a shared life. Physically, it causes chronic pelvic pain, dyspareunia, bowel and bladder symptoms, and fatigue. Psychologically, it generates higher rates of anxiety and depression, anticipatory patterns, and long-term effects from years of medical dismissal. Relationally, it's associated with higher rates of partnership conflict and separation thoughts, with pain and sexual dissatisfaction as the strongest drivers. Financially, it reduces work capacity and accumulates costs that are easy to underestimate. Socially, its invisibility creates a secondary burden of explanation and skepticism that both partners face. Comorbidities including adenomyosis, interstitial cystitis, and pelvic floor dysfunction often co-present and require their own attention. Hugo had spent a year adapting to a life he hadn't fully named. Naming it, which is what this chapter does, is where the more deliberate navigation starts.

Chapter 3: Reading the Flare -- What Is Actually Happening in Her Body

Felix woke at two in the morning to find the other side of the bed empty.

He lay still for a moment listening to the flat. The bathroom door was closed. He got up and stood outside it and said her name quietly.

Paloma said: I'm fine, go back to bed.

He didn't. He sat down on the floor with his back against the wall, in the hallway, a meter from the closed door, and said nothing.

After maybe twenty minutes the door opened. Paloma was sitting with her knees drawn to her chest, back against the side of the bath, and she looked at him without surprise. She said: you didn't have to stay.

He said: I know.

He went in and sat down next to her on the cold tile. He put his arm around her and she leaned into him and they stayed like that for a while. He didn't ask how bad it was. He didn't offer advice. He didn't tell her she should take something. He sat with her while her body did what it was doing, and when it started to ease, a little, she said: you can go back to bed now.

He went. She came back to bed an hour later.

The next morning she told him that sitting with her had been the right thing. He said he didn't know why. She said she didn't entirely either, except that knowing someone was there, without expectation, mattered in a way that was difficult to explain.

He'd been with Paloma for three years by then. He still didn't fully understand what happened in her body during those nights. He knew it was bad. He didn't know why it was bad. He didn't know what made some flares worse than others, or whether what he did or didn't do in the hours before made any difference.

The principle of this chapter is this: a flare makes complete sense once you understand what your partner's body is actually doing. Much of the helplessness that partners feel during a pain episode comes from mystery. Knowledge doesn't stop the flare, but it removes the helplessness. You can't fix what's happening. But you can understand it, and understanding it changes everything about how you're present while it happens.

What Triggers a Flare

Triggers vary between individuals, which is one of the reasons endometriosis flares can seem unpredictable to partners. But they're not random. Most fall into one of several categories, and many women can identify their own pattern with some observation over time.

Menstrual cycle timing is the most consistent trigger. The days around menstruation are typically the highest-risk period for severe pain, because the hormonal cascade that drives menstruation also drives the inflammatory response in endometriotic tissue. For women with deep infiltrating endometriosis or bowel involvement, the days immediately before and during menstruation may be consistently severe.

Physical exertion, particularly exercise that increases intra-abdominal pressure, can trigger or worsen pelvic pain. Running, impact exercise, and heavy lifting can all provoke symptoms, though the relationship isn't universal. Some women find that moderate exercise reduces pain through anti-inflammatory effects. Others find that anything strenuous is a trigger. Knowing which applies takes time and attention.

Diet and digestive state play a role in endometriosis pain, partly through the bowel involvement many women experience. Inflammatory foods, alcohol, and foods that cause bloating or cramping can worsen pelvic symptoms, particularly in the pre-menstrual window. This doesn't mean endometriosis is a dietary condition or that diet can substitute for medical treatment. It means that what she eats in the days before her period matters more than it might for someone without the condition.

Stress activates systemic inflammatory pathways. For a condition that is fundamentally inflammatory, sustained psychological stress can lower the threshold for a pain episode. Paloma could predict a worse-than-usual month if she'd had a high-stress work period. Felix had initially read this as psychosomatic. It's not. It's physiology.

Post-coital pain, pain after sex, can trigger a flare for women with pelvic involvement. Deep penetration or positions that place pressure on the pouch of Douglas, the space between the uterus and rectum, are common triggers for women with posterior endometriosis. This is addressed further in Chapter 7.

What Happens in Her Body During a Flare

Understanding the biology of a pain episode is genuinely useful. It's not academic. It changes how you sit with someone who's in pain.

During menstruation, the uterus contracts to expel its lining. These contractions are driven by prostaglandins, inflammatory signaling molecules released in response to falling progesterone levels. In women without endometriosis, this process produces the cramps associated with a typical period. In women with endometriosis, two things happen simultaneously that intensify this process.

First, the endometriotic tissue outside the uterus responds to the same hormonal signals. It also attempts to break down and bleed. Because it has nowhere to go, it bleeds locally into the surrounding tissue, triggering an acute inflammatory response in the pelvic cavity. The immune system responds to this local bleeding as it would respond to any tissue injury: with inflammation, prostaglandin release, and local swelling.

Second, years of repeated inflammation can sensitize the nerves in the pelvic region. This is called peripheral sensitization, and it means the nervous system has become, over time, more responsive to pain signals in that area. This sensitization is a documented feature of chronic pelvic pain conditions and partly explains why pain doesn't necessarily decrease proportionally with treatment, and why some women continue to experience significant pain even when imaging shows minimal active disease (Morotti et al., 2017).

What you're witnessing during a flare is her body in a genuine physiological crisis. Not an overreaction. Not catastrophizing. Her uterus is contracting. Her pelvic tissue is inflamed. Her nervous system is sending high-intensity pain signals that are calibrated by years of sensitization. The severity of what she's experiencing is real, measurable, and appropriate to what's happening in her body.

> **Teaching Point:** *Nerve sensitization in chronic pelvic pain conditions means that the pain is not always proportional to the current inflammation. Years of repeated flares change how the nervous system processes pain signals. This is a documented physiological process, not a psychological one.*

The Pain Spectrum

Not every flare is the same, and understanding the range helps you distinguish between situations that require your response and situations that require medical attention.

At the lower end of the spectrum, a flare might present as a significant increase in pelvic aching, fatigue, and difficulty with normal activities. She may be able to manage with heat, appropriate medication, and rest. She may be able to work from home or manage a limited schedule.

At the higher end, a flare can be incapacitating. She may be unable to stand, sit upright, or perform any normal function. Nausea, vomiting, and faintness are possible at severe pain levels. In some women, flares at this level occur regularly and are the primary reason for repeated time off work and changes to the shared life Hugo and Noemi had been navigating, and that you may recognize.

Between these poles is a wide spectrum. The critical thing to understand is that a severe flare in a woman with endometriosis isn't evidence of weakness or disproportionate response. It's evidence of the severity of the underlying condition.

Why Pain Doesn't Track With Stage

This is one of the most disorienting features of endometriosis for partners to absorb, and one of the most important to internalize.

There is no reliable correlation between the extent of endometriotic disease visible at surgery and the severity of pain symptoms (Vercellini et al., 2007). A woman with Stage 1 endometriosis can be in as much pain, or more, than a woman with Stage 4. The staging system reflects the anatomical spread of the disease. It doesn't measure pain intensity, nerve sensitization, or the degree to which normal life has been disrupted.

What this means for you: don't use the stage as a calibration device for how seriously to take what she describes. Don't think, even privately, that because a previous imaging result showed minimal disease, the pain she's reporting now must be moderate. Her experience of her pain is the most accurate information available. The stage is one piece of data. Her report of her own experience is another, and it's the more clinically significant one.

> **Action Step:** Observation Challenge: Over the next two weeks, without commenting to her, make a note each day of what you observe: her energy level, whether she mentioned any pain, any activities she avoided, any sleep disruption. At the end of two weeks, look at the pattern. Does it track with her cycle? Are there days that precede the worst ones where something shifts? This kind of observation takes you from reactive to prepared.

The Difference Between Routine and Urgent

Knowing when a flare warrants emergency attention is one of the most practically useful things a partner can learn.

Most flares, even severe ones, are managed at home with heat, appropriate medication, rest, and the kind of presence Felix provided on the bathroom floor. They're not medical emergencies. They're painful and debilitating, but they follow a pattern she and her medical team have established.

The situations that warrant calling a healthcare provider, or in some cases attending emergency care, are these: pain that is significantly worse than her established baseline, particularly if it's acute and sudden rather than gradual. Fever alongside pelvic pain. Vomiting that isn't controlled and that's preventing her from keeping fluids down for an extended period. Difficulty urinating or a complete inability to urinate. Any symptom that she herself describes as different in character from her usual flares.

The key word is different. You're not trying to judge whether her pain is serious. It is serious. You're trying to notice whether it's different from what you know is her pattern. If she says this feels like more than the usual thing, believe her and act on it.

The Emotional Overlay

A flare doesn't only involve the body. It involves everything the body carries.

Anticipatory anxiety in endometriosis is well documented and can amplify the experience of pain before and during a flare. She may begin to feel anxious days before she expects her period, dreading what she knows is coming. During a flare, the anxiety and the pain create a mutually reinforcing cycle: pain increases anxiety, anxiety lowers the pain threshold, the pain gets worse.

She may also feel shame. This is a consequence of years of medical and social invalidation. Many women with endometriosis have internalized a message that their pain is excessive, that it's inconvenient, that they're causing problems by having it. A flare can activate that shame even when there's nothing shameful happening. She's not failing. Her body is in a disease state.

And she may feel grief. A bad flare means another day lost. Another plan cancelled. Another version of herself, the one without pain, that she has to set aside. Partners sometimes underestimate this grief because it's quiet and it doesn't announce itself. It accumulates. Over months and years, it becomes significant.

Felix had noticed, over three years, that Paloma became quieter in the two days before a bad flare. Not withdrawn exactly, just turned slightly inward. He'd learned not to ask "are you okay" because the answer was always "fine," which wasn't dishonest so much as reflexive. He'd learned instead to just be more available in those days, to ask simpler questions and make lighter demands. She hadn't explicitly told him to do this. He'd figured it out by watching. That kind of attention is a form of advocacy too.

The Fine Yesterday Phenomenon

One of the things partners say most often, sometimes unaware of how it lands, is some version of "but you seemed fine yesterday.'"

It's not malicious. It comes from genuine bewilderment. Chronic conditions with episodic severity look inconsistent from the outside. One day she's making dinner and laughing and seems like herself, and the next day she can't get out of bed. From inside the experience, this makes complete sense. From outside it, without the biological framework, it can seem inexplicable.

When a partner says "but you seemed fine yesterday," what she hears is: I don't believe the pain is as bad as you say, because you weren't this bad yesterday. She may not say this aloud. She's probably said it, or thought it, many times and been too tired to have the conversation again.

The biological framework helps here. The pain isn't consistent because the inflammatory state isn't consistent. It fluctuates with the cycle, with triggers, with stress, with the day-to-day variation in her body's inflammatory response. A good day isn't evidence that the bad days aren't bad. It's evidence that the condition is episodic. Those are different things.

Felix had made the "you seemed fine yesterday" comment once, early on, when Paloma had called in sick the morning after an evening when she'd seemed relatively okay. She'd looked at him in a way he hadn't been able to interpret, and hadn't responded. Later, much later, she'd told him what that look was. It was the look she used when she'd decided explaining would cost more than staying quiet. He'd never made that comment again.

> **Action Step:** Action Step: The Flare Baseline Document Create a shared document, digital or paper, that captures: her typical flare triggers in order of

> reliability; her best relief strategies ranked by how often they help; her preference for company versus space during a flare; the specific threshold at which she wants you to suggest calling a healthcare provider; and any language she'd like you to use or avoid when she's in pain. Build this document together during a pain-free day. Review it once a year or after any significant change in her management plan.

In Summary

Flares are driven by a real, physiologically documented process: prostaglandin release during menstruation, inflammatory response from endometriotic tissue bleeding into the pelvic cavity, and nerve sensitization built up over years of repeated episodes. They're triggered by cycle timing, physical exertion, diet, stress, and sometimes by sex. Their severity doesn't track reliably with disease stage. They carry an emotional layer, including anticipatory anxiety, shame, and grief, that compounds the physical experience. The fine yesterday phenomenon is bewildering from outside but biologically explicable. Most flares are managed at home; knowing the signs that warrant medical attention is part of your preparation. Being present without trying to fix is, as Felix learned on a cold bathroom floor, often more useful than anything else.

Chapter 4: The Flare Playbook -- Your Role from Hour One

Mateo was standing outside the bedroom door at ten at night with a heat pad in his hands, not knowing whether to knock.

Lucia had said earlier, when the pain had started coming in: I might just need to be by myself tonight. He'd said okay. He'd made her tea she hadn't touched and tidied the kitchen and answered some emails and now he was standing outside the door trying to decide whether to knock or leave the heat pad by the door or go to the spare room and wait.

He texted her instead. Heat pad out here if you want it. I'll leave it by the door. Let me know if you need anything.

Two minutes later she texted back: Can you come in?

He went in. The room was dark. She was curled on her side with a pillow pressed against her stomach. He sat on the edge of the bed and she said, without looking at him: not to do anything. Just to be here.

He sat on the floor with his back against the bed. He turned his phone face down. He stayed.

Two hours later she said you can go to bed now. He went. She fell asleep soon after.

He thought about it the next morning, trying to work out what he'd actually done, and he couldn't identify anything specific. He'd brought a heat pad. He'd texted instead of knocked. He'd sat on the floor in a dark room for two hours without doing anything useful. And somehow that had been right.

The principle of this chapter: during a flare, the question worth asking yourself is not what can I do to fix this? The answer to that question is nothing. The question worth asking is am I trying to fix this, or am I trying to be present? The research on partner responses to chronic pain is consistent on this point. Partners who prioritize presence over problem-solving are rated significantly more helpful by patients. Partners who attempt to resolve the pain, minimize it, or move past it quickly are rated less so, even when their intentions are good (Cano et al., 2009).

The First Thirty Minutes

The earliest phase of a flare is when partners most reliably make things worse. Not from cruelty but from urgency. Watching someone in pain creates a strong impulse toward action. The problem is that most available actions aren't what she needs.

The most useful thing in the first thirty minutes is presence without expectation. Be in the room, or adjacent to it. Let her know you're there. Don't demand a response or a report on how bad it is. Don't begin generating solutions unless she asks for them.

Language matters here. There's a difference between asking "what do you need?" which places a decision-making burden on her at a moment when she has very limited capacity for decision-making, and saying "I'm here, let me know if anything would help." The second doesn't require anything from her. It just confirms you're present.

Similarly, there's a difference between staying silently present and staying while visibly frustrated. She can tell if you're watching the clock. She can tell if you're sighing. She can tell if the quality of your presence is reluctant. This is not a criticism: it's genuinely hard to sit with someone in pain and feel useless. But the perception that you're suffering through the flare alongside her, as a burden rather than a choice, adds to her emotional load during an already difficult experience.

> **Teaching Point:** *The first thing to manage during a flare isn't her pain. It's your response to it. A partner who is calm and present without agenda gives her something she can't give herself in that moment: a stable environment in which to be in pain without also managing your feelings about it.*

Heat Therapy and Practical Relief

Heat application is one of the most consistently effective self-management tools for menstrual and pelvic pain. The physiological mechanism is well established: heat increases blood flow to the area, relaxes smooth muscle contractions, and reduces prostaglandin activity (Jo & Lee, 2018). For many women with endometriosis, heat is the most reliable immediate relief option available.

Practical heat options: a reusable heat pad or wheat bag heated in the microwave for the lower abdomen. A hot water bottle with a cover, placed over the lower back and lower abdomen. A warm bath, particularly useful for whole-body relaxation alongside pelvic pain relief. TENS machines, which use mild electrical pulses to interrupt pain signaling, have a growing evidence base for chronic pelvic pain and some women find them significantly helpful.

Know where her heat pad is before you need it. Know how she likes it applied: some women want it on the lower abdomen, some on the lower back, some alternate. Know whether she runs warm or cold during flares, because some women find heat intolerable on a hot day even when the pain is severe.

One practical note: have a backup. Heat pads fail, wheat bags lose their warmth, hot water bottles spring leaks. A relationship that has been navigating flares for more than a year probably needs two heat options in the house. This sounds minor. At 2 AM when the first option isn't working and she's in pain, it isn't minor.

Felix had learned to start the kettle the moment Paloma's cycle entered its high-risk window. He didn't wait to be asked. He filled the wheat bag and left it accessible. The act of preparation, of being ready before the crisis, communicated something different from scrambling to find the heat pad after she was already in pain.

Medication Awareness

You don't need to become her pharmacist. You do need to know what she's been prescribed, in broad terms, and what role, if any, you play in that process.

Most women with diagnosed endometriosis have some combination of analgesics available. Non-steroidal anti-inflammatory drugs, NSAIDs, like ibuprofen and naproxen, are first-line for menstrual pain because they work by suppressing the prostaglandin pathway that drives uterine contractions. Taken at full therapeutic dose before the pain peaks, they're significantly more effective than taken reactively. If she's not already timing her NSAIDs to get ahead of the pain rather than chasing it, that's a conversation worth having with her GP.

Some women are prescribed stronger analgesics for severe flare days. Some use hormonal treatments to suppress menstruation and reduce flare frequency and severity. The specific regimen is between her and her medical team. Your role is to know the basics: what she takes, when, at what dose, and whether there are any medications she's been told to avoid.

Don't push medication she hasn't asked for. Don't suggest she "try something stronger" unless she's opened that conversation. Don't imply that if she'd taken something earlier the flare would be less severe. She knows her medication better than you do. Your job is to support the plan she already has, not to second-guess it.

> **Action Step:** Behavior Challenge: This week, before her next high-risk cycle window, find out or review: where her heat pad is. What medications she has available and when she typically takes them. Whether she prefers you in the room or nearby-but-not-in. Whether she wants you to handle external communications, like cancelling plans, or whether she prefers to do that herself. Write it down. You now have the beginnings of a Flare Response Plan.

The Next Several Hours

Once the immediate crisis is managed, the hours that follow are about environment, not intervention.

Manage the home environment so that she doesn't have to think about it. Quiet is usually better than background noise. Low light is usually better than bright. If there are decisions that need making, about dinner, about plans, about anything, make them yourself or defer them. Don't present her with choices she has to weigh when she's in pain and fatigued.

Food and hydration: offer something light and non-demanding. Not a project. Toast, broth, crackers, whatever she can manage without effort. Keep water accessible. Don't make food a complex decision: one suggestion, take it or leave it.

External communications: this is where many partners can make a significant practical contribution. Cancelling plans. Notifying people that she won't make it. Handling work logistics if she's asked you to. She may or may not want you to manage these for her, but asking and being ready to take them over is useful in itself.

The Multi-Day Flare

Some flares last hours. Others last days. When a flare extends across two, three, or more days, the relational and practical demands shift.

Household responsibilities need redistributing. For the duration of the flare, you're managing more. This isn't a sacrifice requiring acknowledgment. It's a practical reality. The partner who takes on household management during a flare without commentary, without a record of favors owed, and without visible resentment gives her the space to rest without guilt.

Your own work and commitments need managing too. A multi-day flare may require changes to your schedule. Some of these are straightforward. Others are harder. The longer you've been in this relationship, the more practiced you'll become at the advance planning that makes these disruptions less disruptive: knowing which of your commitments are flexible, which aren't, and what to say to the people affected by a last-minute change.

Mateo had learned to build what he privately called a buffer day into the week around Lucia's most reliable high-risk window. Not a day off, exactly. A day with no commitments he couldn't rearrange. It had taken two years of trial and error to develop this habit. It was, he'd eventually realized, one of the most useful things he'd done.

The buffer day isn't about resignation. It's about the difference between being caught out and being prepared. When the flare arrives on the day you'd left clear, you can be fully present for it. When it arrives on a day packed with things that can't move, you're managing two crises instead of one, and she can feel the difference.

The second year of this adaptation is usually more functional than the first. By then you've identified the pattern, you've failed a few times in ways that taught you something, and you've built the habits that work for your specific situation. The goal of this chapter is to compress that learning. You don't need a year to develop the buffer day habit. You can decide on it this week.

What Not to Do

This section is specific, because the harmful responses tend to be specific. They're not dramatic. They're the quiet things that compound over time.

Don't ask "how much longer?" It isn't information she has. It also communicates something she'll hear as: I'm waiting for this to be over. The flare is already happening. Your waiting is already happening. Naming it adds nothing except to make her feel like a problem with a duration.

Don't offer unsolicited treatment ideas. You may have read something about a supplement, a diet change, a positioning technique, a yoga approach, or something a friend mentioned. Unless she asks, the flare is not the moment. At best it's irrelevant. At worst, it implies that if she'd tried the right thing earlier, this would be less bad.

Don't minimize. "It can't be that bad" and "it's not a nine, you'd be screaming if it was a nine" are two of the most frequently reported harmful phrases from partner research. Both are empirically wrong. People respond to severe pain very differently. Both are experienced as invalidating. Don't use them.

Don't clock-watch visibly. She can see the phone face up. She notices when you check the time. Even if you're not saying anything, the visible awareness of duration communicates reluctance.

Don't take the flare personally. "This always happens when we have plans" may be true. It's also irrelevant. Endometriosis doesn't schedule around convenience. If the timing consistently feels personal, that's worth examining in yourself, privately, not aloud to her when she's in pain.

Don't bring your own pain into the room unless she asks. "My back is pretty bad too" is well-meaning if you're trying to share the experience. She hears it as competition. She's in a disease state that you're not in. The situations aren't comparable and she knows it, which means any attempt at equivalence lands as minimizing rather than connecting.

The harmful responses are almost never dramatic. They're small and cumulative. A sigh here. A comment there. The visible check of the time. They build up into a pattern she learns to anticipate, and the anticipation of your reluctance becomes something she manages on top of managing the pain. The goal is to be the person whose presence costs her nothing.

> **Action Step:** Writing Challenge: Write down the last thing you said during a flare that didn't land well. Not to beat yourself up over it. To see it clearly. What were you trying to communicate? What might she have heard instead? This kind of reflection, done privately and honestly, is how the helpful fixer learns to become the helpful presence.

When to Escalate

Most flares are managed at home. Some require medical attention. Knowing the difference is important.

Call a healthcare provider or go to emergency care if she reports pain that is significantly worse than her established baseline and is not responding to her usual management. Fever alongside pelvic pain. Vomiting that isn't being controlled and that's preventing her from staying hydrated. Difficulty urinating or complete inability to urinate. Any symptom she describes as different in character from her usual flares.

The last point bears repeating. You're not trying to judge whether the pain is serious. It is serious. You're trying to notice whether it's different from her pattern. If she says this feels like more than usual, treat that as clinically significant information and act accordingly.

In Summary

During a flare, presence outperforms problem-solving. The most useful first response is being in the room or nearby, available without expectation, without a visible investment in how quickly the situation resolves. Heat application is evidence-based and highly effective for many women: know where her heat pad is before you need it, and have a backup. Medication awareness means knowing what she takes, when, and at what dose, and supporting that plan rather than second-guessing it. Over several hours, manage the environment, handle external communications she can't manage, and keep food and hydration accessible without fuss. Multi-day flares require household redistribution without commentary. The harmful responses are specific: asking "how much longer," offering unsolicited remedies, minimizing the pain, clock-watching visibly, taking the timing personally. Most flares are home-managed; a sudden, atypical, or worsening pain pattern warrants medical attention. Mateo's floor moment taught him that being present without agenda is a skill. It's one of the most useful skills in this book. It can be learned.

Chapter 5: The Surgeon's Table -- Understanding Treatment and Supporting Her Through It

Sebastian had been in the hospital car park for two hours when the surgeon came out to find him.

He'd read the pre-operative information sheet three times. He'd been in the consultation with Coralie when the surgical plan was discussed. He'd nodded in what he hoped were the right places. He'd signed something, or perhaps she had, and driven her to the hospital that morning at six-thirty and handed her bag in at the desk and watched her walk through the double doors and sat down in the waiting room and then been unable to sit any longer and moved to the car park.

The surgeon's name was on the consent form. Sebastian couldn't have told you what the procedure was called, specifically. He knew it was a laparoscopy. He'd looked the word up on his phone in the car park and read three different explanations and come away uncertain whether they were describing the same thing.

When the surgeon came out and said Coralie did very well, we found extensive disease and we were able to excise most of it, Sebastian nodded as though he understood the word "excise" in a surgical context.

He drove Coralie home. She slept most of the way. He didn't ask about the surgery because he didn't know what questions to ask, and she was half-sedated. By the evening she was more awake, and she tried to tell him what the surgeon had said, and he realized how little he had with which to receive that information.

The principle of this chapter: surgery is not the end of the endometriosis story. It's a chapter in it. Knowing what kind of surgery she's having, the clinical difference between the two main approaches, and what your role looks like before and after the procedure changes everything about how you're useful through it. Sebastian wasn't prepared. You can be.

The Treatment Hierarchy

Medical management of endometriosis typically moves through a hierarchy of interventions, usually from least invasive to most. Understanding where surgery sits in that hierarchy, and why, helps you have intelligent conversations about her treatment plan.

First-line management is typically analgesic and hormonal. NSAIDs for pain relief. Hormonal treatments, combined oral contraceptives, progesterone-only treatments, GnRH agonists, to suppress menstruation and reduce the estrogen-driven growth of endometriotic tissue. These approaches manage symptoms. They don't remove disease.

When hormonal management fails to adequately control symptoms, or when a patient wants to improve fertility, or when disease is severe enough to cause organ compromise, surgery becomes the appropriate next step. Surgery has two main forms in endometriosis management, and they're not equivalent.

Ablation Versus Excision: The Most Important Distinction

This is the single most clinically significant thing a partner of someone with endometriosis can understand about surgical treatment. The difference between ablation and excision is the difference between a treatment with high recurrence rates and one with significantly lower ones.

Ablation, also called fulguration or coagulation, destroys endometriotic lesions using heat, laser, or electrical current applied to their surface. It's a faster procedure, more widely available, and can be performed by most gynaecological surgeons. It's the most common first surgical approach in many healthcare systems. The problem with ablation is that it treats only the visible surface of the lesion. The deeper tissue, including the root of the lesion, is left behind. Recurrence after ablation is common. Many women experience a return of symptoms within one to three years.

Excision, also called wide local excision, surgically cuts out the lesion from the surrounding tissue. It requires more specialist surgical skill than simple surface destruction and is typically performed by surgeons with specific endometriosis training. It can take longer. Current guidelines and reviews distinguish excision from ablation, but the comparative evidence is not strong enough to support a blanket claim that excision is always superior for every patient or every lesion type (Bafort et al., 2020; ESHRE, 2022).

If Coralie had had ablation previously, and her symptoms had returned, this is the relevant question to ask at any new surgical consultation: is this excision, or ablation? Many patients don't know which they had. Many aren't told the difference. If she's had surgery before and still has symptoms, finding out which approach was used is one of the most practically useful things you can do.

> **Teaching Point:** *The ESHRE 2022 guidelines on endometriosis, the most authoritative clinical reference document in the field, recommend excision over ablation for endometriotic lesions wherever technically feasible. This recommendation is frequently not followed in practice due to lack of specialist access. Knowing this gives you a specific question to ask.*

The Pre-Operative Period: Your Role

In the weeks before surgery, your role is primarily practical and emotional. The surgery itself happens to her, not to you. Your preparation is about making the experience less burdensome for her and less chaotic for you.

Practical preparation for the pre-operative period: know the logistics of the day itself. What time does she need to arrive, who's responsible for transportation, what she needs to bring, what the fasting instructions are. Most laparoscopies are day procedures: she'll go home the same day. Make sure the car is ready, the route is known, and there's someone, which is you, available to stay with her for the first 24 to 48 hours.

Home preparation in the days before surgery: prepare the recovery environment in advance. Clean bedding. Light, easily prepared food in the house. Her medications accessible. A supply of heat pads. If there are stairs she'll need to navigate, think about whether she can stay on a single floor for the first few days. Make sure she has what she needs within reach without having to ask or move around.

Emotional preparation: the night before surgery is often when fear peaks. She may be worrying about what they'll find, about the pain, about recovery, about what comes after. Your role isn't to talk her out of the fear. It's to be present alongside it. You can acknowledge the fear without trying to resolve it.

A simple thing that partners consistently report being useful: ask her what would be most helpful tonight. Some women want to be distracted. Some want to talk about what they're afraid of. Some want practical company, a film, a walk, something that keeps them occupied without requiring much. Ask, then follow through on what she says. The night before surgery is not the moment to guess.

What Happens on the Day

A laparoscopy is performed under general anesthesia. The surgeon makes two to four small incisions in the abdomen, typically under a centimeter each. The abdomen is inflated with carbon dioxide gas to create space for the surgical instruments and the camera. The laparoscope, a thin camera, is inserted through one incision. The surgical instruments are inserted through the others.

The surgery can last anywhere from thirty minutes to several hours, depending on the extent of disease and whether excision is being performed. If she's having excision of deep infiltrating endometriosis with bowel involvement, the procedure can be significantly longer and may involve colorectal surgeons alongside the gynecological team.

In the recovery room after surgery, she'll wake gradually from general anesthesia. She may be disoriented, nauseous, or tearful. The tearfulness is a known response to emerging from general anesthesia: it isn't necessarily emotional in origin, though it can become so. Don't try to interpret everything she says or does in the first hour out of surgery. Her brain is coming back online.

In the waiting room: there's nothing useful you can do. You know this. Bring something to read. Don't repeatedly ask the desk for updates. When the surgeon finds you to report on the procedure, ask for clarification on anything you don't understand. You're entitled to know what was found and what was done, and a surgeon who is used to operating on this patient knows you're there to support her.

Recovery: The Timeline

Post-operative recovery from laparoscopy follows a general pattern, though it varies between individuals and depends significantly on the extent of the surgery.

The first 48 to 72 hours: she'll be home the same day in most cases. She'll be fatigued from the anesthesia, which typically takes 24 to 48 hours to fully clear. She'll have some abdominal pain at the incision sites and internally. She should rest. Light liquids, then soft foods when she can manage them. No driving. No lifting. No strenuous activity.

The first two weeks: gradual increase in activity, led by how she feels. Light walking within a few days. A return to desk work within one to two weeks for most women. Driving typically cleared at two weeks, though this varies by surgeon. Continued fatigue is normal and should be accommodated, not pushed through.

Full recovery: typically four to six weeks for most laparoscopic procedures. Return to normal exercise at around four weeks, guided by her surgeon. Return to penetrative sex at four to six weeks, which is addressed in Chapter 7.

Sebastian had expected Coralie to be essentially recovered within a week. She wasn't. Her fatigue persisted for three weeks. He'd found this harder to navigate than the immediate post-operative period, because it was less dramatic and therefore harder to justify. But fatigue after excision surgery is real, documented, and appropriate to the surgical experience.

Symptoms Partners Misread as Complications

The most common source of post-operative panic for partners is the referred shoulder pain that occurs in the first 24 to 72 hours after laparoscopy. It can be alarming if you're not expecting it.

The carbon dioxide gas used to inflate the abdomen doesn't fully evacuate after the procedure. What remains gets absorbed and rises, collecting against the diaphragm. The diaphragm is innervated by the phrenic nerve, which also innervates the shoulder. The result is pain referred to the shoulder and sometimes neck, which can feel completely disconnected from the procedure that caused it. It's very common. It's not dangerous. It typically resolves within 24 to 48 hours. Heat applied to the shoulder helps. Moving slowly and gently helps.

Incision site bruising is normal. Mild abdominal bloating is normal. The abdomen will remain tender for days to weeks, particularly around the incision sites. Mood variability in the first week is normal and often significant: the combination of general anesthesia, hormonal fluctuations triggered by the surgery, physical pain, and the emotional weight of confirmation of disease can produce a period of genuine emotional instability that isn't always flagged in pre-operative information.

The Emotional Recovery

This phase is the one most partners underestimate, because it isn't on the recovery timeline they receive from the surgical team.

Many women experience a complicated emotional response in the weeks after surgery. There's often relief, sometimes profound relief, at having the disease confirmed and addressed. There's often grief, because what was found was more extensive than hoped, or because the procedure confirmed what years of dismissal had denied. There's often uncertainty, because endometriosis can recur, because excision isn't a cure, because the question of what comes next hasn't been answered.

Don't rush her through this. Don't assume that because the surgery went well, the emotional processing should be complete within a week. Don't project relief onto her if what she's actually feeling is grief. Ask, carefully and without agenda, how she's doing with what was found.

Sebastian had made this mistake. In the first week after Coralie's excision surgery, he'd been relentlessly optimistic. He'd spoken about what they'd do once she was recovered. He'd talked about plans. He hadn't noticed that she kept going quiet when he did this, until she said, gently, that she wasn't ready to talk about afterward yet. She was still in the middle of processing what had been found. The optimism he'd meant as encouragement was landing as pressure to get past the surgery rather than through it.

He'd learned to ask instead of predict. What's going through your head today? Not: when do you think you'll be feeling better? The first question opens the door. The second closes it.

> **Action Step:** Conversation Challenge: In the first week after surgery, choose a quiet moment when she seems relatively comfortable. Ask one question that isn't about her physical recovery. Not "how's the pain today" but something more like: "what's been going through your head this week?" Then listen. Don't solve. Don't reframe toward optimism. Let her tell you what the experience is actually like from where she's standing.

Recurrence: What It Means

Endometriosis can and does recur after surgery. This is a feature of the condition, not a failure of the surgeon or the patient. Recurrence rates after excision are lower than after ablation, but they're not zero. If her symptoms return months or years after surgery, the framework you've built in these chapters applies again.

The emotional weight of recurrence is significant. Many women describe a particular kind of grief when symptoms return: the renewed hope of the post-surgical period, the adaptation to a different life, and then the slow reappearance of familiar pain. This cycle can be more devastating than the first diagnosis.

As a partner, you may also feel grief at recurrence. You'd perhaps begun to imagine the life on the other side of surgery.

You'd been allowing yourself to hope. When symptoms return, that hope takes a blow, and it's okay to feel that. What matters is where you put that grief. Not into frustration that lands on her. Not into a visible withdrawing. Into honest acknowledgment between you, if she's in a place to hear it, or into your own support structures if she isn't.

Your role is to stay steady. Recurrence isn't a reason to catastrophize, to catastrophize about the future of her fertility, or to catastrophize about the relationship. It's a clinical event with a management pathway. The same advocacy skills that got her to the right surgeon the first time are the same skills that will serve you in the second cycle.

In Summary

Treatment for endometriosis moves through a hierarchy from hormonal management to surgery. The two main surgical approaches are ablation, which destroys the surface of lesions and carries higher recurrence rates, and excision, which removes lesions in their entirety and is preferred by ESHRE 2022 guidelines. Knowing which approach she's had, or is being offered, is one of the most practically useful pieces of clinical literacy a partner can carry. The pre-operative period is yours to manage: logistics, home preparation, and being present for the night before. Surgery day is a waiting room experience. Recovery follows a timeline of 48 to 72 hours for immediate recovery, two weeks for return to desk work, and four to six weeks for full activity. Referred shoulder pain from CO2 gas is common, harmless, and alarming if you're not expecting it. Emotional recovery takes longer than physical recovery.

Recurrence is a clinical reality, not a failure. The same preparation that served you the first time will serve you again.

Chapter 6: Becoming Her Advocate -- Navigating the Healthcare System

Julian had been in the consultation room for forty minutes, sitting slightly behind Valeria and to the left, the way you sit when you're not sure whether your presence is welcome.

The consultant was polite. He was thorough in a way that felt careful rather than engaged. He reviewed Valeria's symptom history with the kind of facial neutrality that Julian had learned, over three years, to distrust. When Valeria described the pain in the weeks after her last cycle, he nodded and said: yes, that pattern is quite typical. There are a few options we might consider. Let's see how you get on over the next couple of months and then review.

Valeria nodded.

Julian watched her face. He knew that nod. It was the nod she used when she'd decided the fight wasn't worth having, when she'd calculated that pushing back would cost more than it returned. He'd watched her produce it in eleven previous appointment rooms.

He had nothing to say. He hadn't prepared anything. He didn't know the right questions. He sat behind her and said nothing, and the appointment ended, and they walked out to the car park.

In the car, Valeria said: I hate myself when I do that.

He said: I should have said something.

She said: I know. But you didn't know what to say.

That was true. And it was the last time it was true.

The principle of this chapter: a partner who walks into the clinic with the right language changes what happens in the room. The available research supports a couple-centered approach: qualitative ENDOPART findings show that partners are often affected across sex and intimacy, fertility planning, work, household income, and emotional wellbeing, yet are commonly left outside care conversations (Culley et al., 2017). The clinical outcome isn't the only thing that changes. The relationship changes too.

Why Advocacy Changes the Relationship

The research on partner involvement in endometriosis care is relatively recent. The ENDOPART study, a qualitative UK study of 22 women with laparoscopically diagnosed endometriosis and their male partners, found that partners often take on support tasks, experience helplessness, frustration, worry, and anger, and lack professional recognition or dedicated support (Culley et al., 2017).

This isn't only because the clinical outcomes were better, though they often were. It's because the act of a partner investing in clinical literacy communicates something to the person with the condition. It says: I take this seriously. I take your experience seriously. You're not navigating this alone.

For women who have spent years being told by medical systems that they were making too much of their symptoms, a partner who takes the symptoms seriously is not a small thing. It's a form of witnessing. And it happens to also produce better practical outcomes in the room.

A Clinical Glossary

These are the terms worth knowing. Not to perform knowledge, but to have a foundation for the conversations that matter.

ASRM staging: the American Society for Reproductive Medicine classification of endometriosis in four stages by extent and adhesion severity. Reviewed in Chapter 1. Stage doesn't predict pain.

ESHRE: the European Society of Human Reproduction and Embryology. The body whose guidelines represent the current consensus on best-practice management of endometriosis in clinical settings. When you ask a consultant whether an approach is consistent with current ESHRE guidance, you're asking a specific, answerable question.

Transvaginal ultrasound: an ultrasound performed via a transducer inserted vaginally. More sensitive than abdominal ultrasound for pelvic assessment. Can detect endometriomas. Cannot reliably detect peritoneal lesions or adhesions.

Pelvic MRI: magnetic resonance imaging of the pelvis. More sensitive than ultrasound for detecting deep infiltrating endometriosis, particularly involving the bowel and bladder. Still cannot definitively diagnose all forms. Not a substitute for laparoscopy.

Diagnostic laparoscopy: the only definitive diagnostic method for endometriosis. A surgical procedure using a camera inserted through small abdominal incisions. Can be combined with treatment at the time of diagnosis.

Excision versus ablation: reviewed in Chapter 5. Excision removes lesions in their entirety. Ablation destroys the surface only. ESHRE 2022 guidelines favor excision.

Adenomyosis: a related condition in which tissue similar to the uterine lining grows within the wall of the uterus itself. Causes heavy periods, cramping, and an enlarged uterus. Diagnosed through ultrasound or MRI. Frequently co-presents with endometriosis.

Pelvic floor dysfunction: hypertonicity, which is chronic contraction and tenderness, of the pelvic floor muscles. Common in women with chronic pelvic pain. Contributes to dyspareunia, bowel and bladder symptoms, and a cycle of pain that persists even when endometriosis is treated. Treated by specialist pelvic floor physiotherapy.

Preparing for an Appointment

Most appointments are too short. The average primary care consultation is under ten minutes. Specialist appointments are longer but rarely long enough. Preparation is the difference between an appointment that moves things forward and one that doesn't.

Before the appointment, help her document: her current symptom pattern, specifically. Not "bad periods" but: pelvic pain rated 7 to 9 out of 10 in the five days before and during menstruation, dyspareunia rated 6 to 8 after penetrative sex, fatigue rated significant on approximately 15 days per cycle, constipation in the week before menstruation. Specific, timed, and cyclical. This kind of documentation makes the symptom pattern harder to minimize.

Bring: any previous imaging reports, any surgical notes from previous procedures, a list of current medications and their dosages, and a single primary question for this appointment. Not a list of fifteen questions. One primary question that represents the most important thing she needs from this visit. Clarity about what you're there for helps the consultation stay on track.

Know the outcome you're seeking before you go in. "We want to discuss whether she's a candidate for excision surgery with a specialist." "We want to understand why her symptoms have returned since the last procedure." "We want a referral to a pelvic floor physiotherapist." Arrive with the destination. The consultation is about how to get there.

> **Teaching Point:** *Women with endometriosis who bring a partner who participates actively in their consultations report that clinicians take their symptom descriptions more seriously. The presence of a second, corroborating witness changes the dynamic in the room.*

Scripts for the Consultation

Scripts feel awkward until you've used them once. Then they feel like the difference between having something to say and having nothing.

Introducing yourself: "I'm Valeria's partner, Julian. She's asked me to be here to help take notes and support the conversation." This establishes your role, positions you as functional rather than merely present, and gives the clinician a reason to address both of you.

When the answer is "let's wait and see": "We've been managing this for three years now and the symptoms have been progressive. What specific outcome would shift the recommendation toward more active investigation? Can you give us a threshold?" This converts a vague recommendation into a specific clinical criterion, which is much harder for a clinician to deflect.

When requesting referral to a specialist: "We understand that deep excision surgery may be outside the scope of this service. Could you refer Valeria to a centre with specialist expertise in endometriosis? We'd like access to a surgeon who routinely operates on this condition." Specific request, specific rationale, specific desired outcome.

After a dismissal or non-answer: "I want to make sure I've understood correctly. The recommendation today is continued monitoring rather than further investigation. I'd like to have that noted in today's clinical record." Clinicians who know that a non-answer is being formally noted sometimes reconsider it.

When she's in pain or too depleted to advocate: "Valeria's finding this appointment very difficult today. I'll be taking notes and asking a few questions on her behalf, with her permission. Is that okay?" Then proceed.

> **Action Step:** Conversation Challenge: Before her next appointment, have a ten-minute conversation the evening before. Ask her: what's the one thing she needs to come out of this appointment having achieved? Then ask: is there anything she'd like you to say, or anything she'd prefer you not to say? Some women want a partner who advocates actively. Some want a partner who witnesses quietly. Knowing which she wants, in advance, is itself a form of advocacy.

Finding a Specialist

Not every gynaecologist is trained in excision surgery. Finding one who is requires specific criteria.

In the United Kingdom, the British Society for Gynaecological Endoscopy maintains a list of accredited endometriosis centres. These are NHS centres assessed against specific clinical criteria for endometriosis management. If she isn't already under the care of one, a referral to a BSGE-accredited centre is worth requesting.

In the United States, the American Association of Gynecologic Laparoscopists lists members with specific interest in endometriosis. The Endometriosis Foundation of America's referral network lists surgeons who perform excision. Nancy's Nook, a patient-community resource, maintains a crowd-sourced list of experienced excision surgeons that many endometriosis patients and partners find more practically useful than official directories.

When evaluating a surgeon's expertise, the questions worth asking are: what proportion of your surgical caseload involves endometriosis? Do you routinely perform excision, or primarily ablation? What's your approach to deep infiltrating endometriosis with bowel involvement? A surgeon with genuine expertise will answer these questions readily. One who deflects or is uncertain is giving you information too.

Insurance and NHS Navigation

Healthcare system navigation is frustrating, specific to context, and often the thing partners are least prepared for.

In NHS contexts: the pathway to specialist referral typically runs through the GP. A letter requesting specialist endometriosis centre referral, citing symptom duration, previous treatments tried, and the specific clinical concern, is more likely to be acted on than a verbal request in a short consultation. If the GP declines to refer, ask for the reasons in writing. If those reasons aren't clinically defensible, they can be challenged through NHS complaints and advocacy pathways.

In insurance-based systems: know what's covered before the appointment. Know whether referrals require pre-authorization. Know whether excision surgery at a specialist centre requires prior approval that ablation at a local facility wouldn't. These are questions to have answered before you're in the room, not after.

In all systems: documentation matters. Request copies of clinical notes after significant appointments. Keep a folder with dates, clinician names, diagnoses made or refused, treatments recommended, and outcomes. This documentation has value in insurance disputes, in second-opinion contexts, and in demonstrating a pattern of inadequate care if formal complaints become necessary.

The documentation habit feels bureaucratic. It is bureaucratic. It's also the kind of preparation that, if you need it, you'll be very glad you did. The couple who arrives at a third specialist with a clean summary of everything that's been tried and failed, and when, and who made what recommendation, is the couple that gets faster action. It's not about being adversarial. It's about replacing the vague with the specific, and a clinician who receives the specific knows they're dealing with someone who has been paying attention. That changes the appointment.

When She Can't Advocate for Herself

There will be appointments where she's too exhausted to fight. Where the pain is bad and she has no reserves for the emotional work of pushing back. Where she nods the way Valeria nodded, and you can see it happening, and you need to be ready.

Ask permission first: "Would it help if I take the lead on the questions today?" This acknowledges her agency even in a moment when she doesn't have capacity to exercise it. Don't override without asking.

Then proceed. Not aggressively. Not in a way that positions her as an invalid who can't speak for herself. But with the specific question prepared, the outcome desired, and the willingness to say clearly: we're not leaving without an answer to this.

After the appointment, debrief without judgment. What did she take from it? What would she have wanted to do differently? What would be useful at the next one? The debrief is a form of calibration. It makes you more useful the next time.

Julian had the conversation with Valeria in the car park. He told her what he should have said. She told him what she'd needed. They drove home and he drafted a letter to the consultant requesting a specific referral, citing the three previous appointments at which conservative management had been recommended without improvement in symptoms. The referral came through four weeks later.

He'd been in that consultation room doing nothing for six months. Then he prepared once, and things moved.

The clinical system isn't the enemy. Most clinicians are doing their best in a system with limited time and heavy patient loads. What the system doesn't have enough of is partners who've read something, who know the right question, who stay calm when they push back. That's the gap you can fill. It's not a dramatic role. It's a prepared one.

> **Action Step:** Behavior Challenge: The Clinic Preparation Template Before her next appointment, prepare a single page that includes: her current symptoms with timing and severity; her current medications and dosages; two or three questions in order of priority; and the one specific outcome you're aiming for from this visit. Bring two copies, one for you and one in case it's useful to hand to the clinician. Review it together the evening before. Having it on paper means neither of you has to hold it all in your head under pressure.

In a Nutshell

A partner who walks into a clinical setting with clinical literacy, a documented symptom history, a specific outcome goal, and ready language for the common responses changes what happens in the room. Research consistently shows that active partner involvement in endometriosis healthcare is associated with better patient psychological outcomes, higher relationship satisfaction, and better dyadic coping. The clinical vocabulary worth knowing: ASRM staging, ESHRE guidelines, the diagnostic tools and their limits, excision versus ablation, adenomyosis, pelvic floor dysfunction. Appointment preparation means a documented symptom history, previous records, current medications, and one primary outcome goal. Scripts for common situations: introducing yourself, responding to "let's wait and see," requesting specialist referral, and formally noting a non-answer. Finding a specialist means seeking excision-trained surgeons through BSGE accreditation in the UK, AAGL and Nancy's Nook in the US. When she can't advocate, ask permission to lead, then lead well. The documentation habit takes five minutes after each appointment and can matter enormously later. Julian had been in eleven consultation rooms before he was prepared for the twelfth. You can be prepared before that.

Chapter 7: The Intimacy Map -- Rebuilding a Sexual and Emotional Connection

Elio knew the shape of the silence. It had texture by now.

They'd been lying next to each other for twenty minutes. The room was dark. Margot was awake. He knew she was awake by the quality of her stillness, the specific kind of not-moving that was different from sleeping. He was awake too, and he wanted to reach over and touch her shoulder and say: can we talk about what's happening between us? But those words felt like an accusation he hadn't intended to make. So he said nothing. She said nothing. They both fell asleep eventually.

In the morning he made coffee and she was warm and kind and nothing was wrong, and nothing was right, and neither of them said a word about any of it.

That was the third month in a row. He'd started keeping count.

The silence around physical intimacy in an endometriosis relationship has a specific quality. It isn't the comfortable quiet of a relationship that doesn't need words. It's the strained quiet of two people who both know something important isn't being said, and who are each protecting the other from the difficulty of saying it. She doesn't raise it because she fears he resents what the pain has taken from their physical life. He doesn't raise it because he doesn't want her to feel guilty about something she can't control. Both are trying to protect the other. Both are lonely.

The principle of this chapter: dyspareunia doesn't end physical intimacy. It redirects it. The couples who rebuild a connected physical life after endometriosis are the ones who stop treating penetrative sex as the destination and start treating physical closeness as the language. The map doesn't disappear. It gets redrawn.

Why Both Partners Go Silent

Research on sexuality in endometriosis partnerships finds that changes to sexual activity are common. A multicenter case-control study in Switzerland, Germany, and Austria found that 75% of male partners of women with endometriosis reported changes in sexuality, while partners in affected couples reported lower sexual satisfaction than control partners (Hämmerli et al., 2018). The avoidance is often bidirectional. Both partners may withdraw for the same reason: the desire not to cause harm.

What neither partner realizes, in most cases, is that the withdrawal from physical contact tends to extend well beyond penetrative sex. Casual touch reduces. Spontaneous affection reduces. Physical proximity during ordinary activities reduces. This happens because both partners begin unconsciously associating physical contact with the possibility of a painful endpoint, and the association spreads across all physical closeness, not only the kind that might lead somewhere.

By the time Elio was keeping count of the silent nights, he and Margot had been in a pattern for about eight months where they barely touched each other outside of brief functional gestures. He hadn't consciously decided to stop. He'd gotten careful, and caution had a logic that extended further than he'd meant it to.

The silence makes things worse, not better. Research on chronic genital and pelvic pain shows that avoidance can maintain anxiety, pain-related fear, and sexual disconnection, although the evidence is stronger for vulvodynia and genito-pelvic pain than for endometriosis alone (Pukall et al., 2016). Careful, honest engagement is usually safer than pretending the problem is not there.

> **Teaching Point:** *The silence around intimacy in an endometriosis relationship isn't a sign that the relationship is failing. It's a sign that both partners care enough to protect each other from their own fears. Understanding this is the first step toward breaking the silence usefully, without blame and without pressure.*

What Dyspareunia Actually Involves

Understanding the physiology of painful sex in endometriosis changes the meaning of the experience for both partners. The most damaging interpretation a partner can carry is that the pain reflects something about her feelings for him. It doesn't. It reflects anatomy.

The most common source of dyspareunia in endometriosis is the direct involvement of lesions in the pouch of Douglas, the space between the uterus and the rectum. Deep penetration compresses or displaces these lesions and the adhesions surrounding them, producing immediate and often severe pain. This is a structural event. It has nothing to do with desire, arousal, trust, or how she feels about the person she's with.

A second major contributor is pelvic floor hypertonicity, introduced in Chapter 2. Years of pelvic pain cause the pelvic floor muscles to contract protectively around the area that hurts.

Over time, those muscles become chronically tense and tender. Penetration into a hypertonic pelvic floor is painful for reasons entirely separate from the endometriosis itself. This is why some women continue to experience dyspareunia after successful excision surgery: the surgical disease has been removed, but the pelvic floor's adaptation to years of pain hasn't resolved on its own.

The third layer is anticipatory. Once penetration has been painful several times, the nervous system learns to expect pain before contact occurs. Arousal may reduce. Muscle bracing may increase. This anticipatory response is a documented neurological process that can make the experience more painful than the underlying biology would produce without it. It is not psychological weakness. It is how nervous systems respond to repeated painful stimuli.

What this means for Elio, and for every partner in this situation: when Margot says sex hurts, she is reporting a physiological event. The pain isn't about desire or connection or how she feels about him. Internalizing this distinction, truly internalizing it, changes what the silence means and makes the conversation that ends it possible.

The Avoidance Cycle and How to Exit It

The avoidance cycle has a predictable shape. A painful experience leads to reduced initiation. Reduced initiation leads to reduced casual physical contact. Reduced physical contact produces emotional distance. The emotional distance makes it harder to have the conversation that would restart the physical connection.

Elio had spent six months in the avoidance cycle before he recognized it as a cycle. He'd thought each step was a reasonable accommodation. The accumulated effect of the steps was a relationship that had become almost entirely non-physical, which was not what either of them had chosen and not what either of them wanted.

The exit from the avoidance cycle doesn't begin with sex. It begins with a conversation, and the conversation begins with one person saying, clearly and without blame, that they've noticed the pattern and want to talk about it.

Elio had that conversation on a Saturday afternoon when they were both well-rested and Margot was in a comfortable phase of her cycle. He said: I've been missing being physically close to you, and I've noticed that I've been pulling back too, partly because I didn't want to put pressure on you. He said he wasn't looking for any particular outcome from the conversation. He just wanted to stop pretending the pattern wasn't there.

Margot cried, briefly, and said: I thought you'd stopped wanting me. That misunderstanding, which both of them had been living inside for months, dissolved in about thirty seconds of honest speech.

This is what the avoidance cycle costs. Not the absence of sex. The absence of the thirty seconds that could dissolve the misunderstanding. Both partners circling a conversation that would take half a minute to have and might change everything, and choosing instead to lie in the dark saying nothing.

> **Action Step:** Conversation Challenge: This week, identify a low-pressure moment and use one of these

> sentences: "I've been missing being physically close to you" or "I think we've both been a bit careful around each other and I'd like to talk about it." Don't set an agenda for what comes next. Just open the door and see what's on the other side of it.

Non-Penetrative Intimacy and Sensate Focus

Sensate focus is a structured approach to physical intimacy developed by Masters and Johnson in the 1960s and refined extensively since, specifically for couples navigating the intersection of chronic pain and physical closeness. Its core principle is deceptively simple: explore physical pleasure together without the expectation of any specific outcome.

In practice, this means two partners take turns touching each other for sensory interest, without pressure toward penetration, orgasm, or any particular endpoint. The person receiving touch gives real-time feedback. The person giving touch stays curious rather than goal-directed. Sessions typically last 20 to 30 minutes. They happen weekly, or at whatever cadence works for the couple.

The clinical literature on couple-based and behavioral approaches for women with chronic pelvic pain supports careful, graded, non-demand physical contact as part of broader treatment, though the evidence is mixed and not specific to every endometriosis presentation (McGuire et al., 2017). The technique works not because it resolves the disease but because it helps rebuild a physical relationship around pain rather than through it.

Margot had first read about sensate focus in preparation for her pelvic floor physiotherapy sessions. She'd come home and explained it to Elio, and he'd felt a little self-conscious about the idea of structured touching. He'd done it anyway. The first session was awkward and the second was less so and the third was the first time they'd genuinely laughed together in a physical context in about a year. The laughter surprised him. He hadn't expected that particular return.

Non-penetrative physical intimacy extends beyond structured sensate focus. Massage. Shared baths or showers. Physical closeness without expectation during films or quiet evenings. Holding each other in the morning before getting up. These acts don't require a clinical framework. They require only the shared decision, made quietly and without pressure, to maintain physical warmth regardless of what's currently possible in terms of sexual activity.

Pelvic Floor Physiotherapy

If she hasn't been referred to a specialist pelvic floor physiotherapist, that referral is worth requesting as a specific priority alongside her endometriosis management. It addresses the dimension of dyspareunia that endometriosis surgery alone doesn't treat.

A pelvic floor physiotherapist treats the muscular and connective tissue contributors to pelvic pain, principally the hypertonicity that accumulates after years of the body bracing against pain. Treatment typically includes manual therapy to address the tension directly, breathing and relaxation work to break the protective bracing pattern, biofeedback to help her develop voluntary control over muscles that have been involuntarily contracted for years, and graduated exercises.

The outcomes for pelvic floor physiotherapy in dyspareunia are documented across multiple clinical studies. Women who complete a course of treatment report significant reductions in pain during intercourse, improved sexual function scores, and better overall pelvic pain management (Berghmans, 2018). It isn't a cure. For many women, it's the piece of the management plan that addresses the physical dimension of the intimacy problem in a way that nothing else does.

Your role in her physiotherapy process: ask if she'd like company for the first appointment. Ask how sessions are going if she wants to talk about them. Some women share the home exercises with their partners because having a partner who understands the exercises makes it easier to do them. Others keep this private. Take her lead. Pelvic floor physiotherapy can be an intimate kind of clinical work and she'll manage the degree of sharing that's comfortable for her.

After Treatment: Rebuilding the Map

Post-surgical intimacy rebuilding follows its own timeline, which is partly physical and partly relational.

After laparoscopy, timing for resuming penetrative sexual activity should come from her surgical team. Many discharge plans use a healing window of several weeks, but the right timing depends on the procedure, complications, bleeding, pain, infection risk, and the surgeon's instructions. Whether either partner feels emotionally ready to re-engage with physical intimacy by that point is a separate question with a separate timeline.

Elio and Margot waited about nine weeks after her excision surgery before attempting anything, and they approached it specifically within a sensate focus framework rather than as a return to previous patterns. What happened was that pain was present but different in character, more manageable, and more limited to specific movements, than it had been before surgery. What also happened was that they had a conversation during rather than afterward, which was something they'd never done before and which changed the quality of the experience significantly.

The map after surgery isn't the map before the diagnosis. It's a new map, built deliberately rather than inherited from the relationship before endometriosis arrived. The couples who report the most satisfying physical lives after diagnosis are the ones who built that new map explicitly, through conversation and sensate focus and pelvic floor physiotherapy and a willingness to take longer to arrive somewhere and say so along the way.

Elio and Margot, eighteen months after her excision surgery, have a physical relationship that is different from what they had in the years before the diagnosis and more intentional. They've had conversations about their physical life that they never had when it didn't require conversation. Margot said once, on a weekend when they'd done a sensate focus session for the first time in two months, that she felt more known physically than she ever had. Elio thought about this for a while afterward. He thought: the diagnosis gave us something, too. Not enough to be grateful for it. But something.

In a Nutshell

The silence around physical intimacy in an endometriosis relationship is nearly universal, bidirectional, and actively harmful over time. Dyspareunia has anatomical sources, including lesions in the pouch of Douglas and pelvic floor hypertonicity, and a neurological anticipatory layer. None of these sources reflect anything about the quality of the relationship. The avoidance cycle extends beyond sexual activity to all physical closeness, which is why the relational cost of avoidance is larger than partners typically expect. Sensate focus offers an evidence-based structure for rebuilding physical intimacy without performance pressure. Pelvic floor physiotherapy addresses the muscular dimension of dyspareunia that surgery alone doesn't treat. The post-surgical intimacy timeline is partly physical and partly relational. Elio's thirty seconds of honest speech dissolved eight months of misunderstanding. The new map is worth building, and it's worth building out loud.

Elio and Margot are a composite case drawn from the patterns consistently described in clinical practice and partner research. The specific details, the silent nights, the sensate focus discovery, the laughter in session three, are drawn from what partners and their therapists describe as the shape of intimacy rebuilding after dyspareunia. The composite is honest: this is what it looks like when it goes well. It goes well when both people decide to stop protecting each other from the conversation and start having it.

Chapter 8: Your Emotional Landscape -- Processing the Partner's Inner Life

Gabriel had been sitting in his car outside the house for twenty-two minutes.

He knew the number because he'd looked at the clock when he parked and again when he finally reached for the door handle. The engine was off. The kitchen light was on. He could see Zoe moving in there, probably making tea, and he watched her through the window and thought: I am not ready to be okay yet.

Nothing catastrophic had happened that day. It had just been another day in a long run of another days, and something in him had used up faster than it was being replaced. He was tired in a way that the weekend hadn't touched. He was patient in a way that was starting to feel like theater.

He hadn't told Zoe about the twenty-two minutes. He hadn't told her about any of the minutes like them. She was carrying something much larger, and this felt smaller, and he'd developed a habit of editing himself before he came through the door. His version of himself that went inside was the composed one, the reliable one, the one who'd made his adjustments and had the things she needed.

He hadn't noticed, until that night, that the editing had a cost.

The principle of this chapter: the partner's emotional experience in an endometriosis relationship is real, layered, and deserves acknowledgment rather than management. Guilt, resentment, anticipatory grief, and compassion fatigue are not signs of inadequate love. They're the predictable responses of a person who has been carrying something substantial for a long period of time without a designated place to put it down. Unprocessed, they accumulate. They surface in the relationship in ways that are harder to manage than the original feelings would have been if they'd been named earlier.

The Guilt-Resentment Loop

The emotional pattern most consistently described by partners of people with endometriosis is a cycle between guilt and resentment that feeds itself and is difficult to exit once it's established.

The cycle runs like this. Something happens: a plan cancelled by a flare, a week where the household management falls entirely to one person again, a holiday that becomes a recovery period instead of what it was supposed to be. Resentment surfaces. It's real and appropriate: a need hasn't been met, a loss has occurred. Almost immediately, guilt follows: she's in pain, how can I feel resentful, what does that say about me? The guilt suppresses the resentment. The resentment doesn't disappear. It accumulates. The next trigger adds to the accumulated store, the guilt returns larger, and the cycle continues.

Both emotions are information. Resentment signals that something isn't sustainable. It isn't a verdict on the relationship or evidence that love has worn thin. Guilt signals that you care about the impact of your resentment. It's evidence of empathy. What makes the loop destructive isn't either emotion individually. It's the refusal to acknowledge either of them, which keeps both of them active and growing in the background.

A 2024 French EndoVie partner survey found that 19% of partners reported feeling guilty about blaming their partner because of endometriosis, and 26% reported that they did not often or very often understand their partner's expectations during endometriosis-associated pain (Santulli et al., 2024). Both figures likely undercount the actual prevalence. People who feel guilty about feelings tend to underreport those feelings, including in surveys.

Gabriel had been in the guilt-resentment loop since about year one. He'd felt resentful about a trip they'd cancelled in their second winter together, and felt guilty about the resentment, and said nothing about either feeling, and by year three was sitting in a car outside his own house unable to go inside because the composite weight of all the unsaid things had become too heavy to carry in through the door.

> **Teaching Point:** *Resentment in a caregiving relationship isn't a moral failing. It's a signal: something isn't sustainable here. The most useful response to that signal isn't suppression. It's honest attention to what the resentment is pointing at.*

Anticipatory Grief

Anticipatory grief is grief for things that haven't been lost yet but may be, or for versions of the future that are no longer certain. It differs from the grief that follows a definite loss in that it has no recognized form and no social scaffold. You haven't lost anything you can name to other people. You're grieving a possibility, and grieving possibilities doesn't come with the rituals or acknowledgment that surround concrete loss.

Partners of people with endometriosis grieve specific things. The relationship as it existed before the diagnosis. The physical intimacy that was present and is now constrained. The holidays that now require contingency planning. The children who may or may not happen. The version of her that existed before the condition took up permanent residence. Each of these is a real loss, or a genuine threat of loss, and the grief that surrounds them is appropriate.

Gabriel had grieved the backpacking trips. That was the specific one. He and Zoe had planned, in the early days before the diagnosis, to do one long wilderness trip each year. They'd done one. He'd quietly stopped planning the next one when the endometriosis made the logistics genuinely uncertain, and then stopped planning the one after that, and the quiet stopping was a grief that hadn't been named. When he finally named it, to a therapist in year three, he cried in a way that surprised him. Not for the trips specifically but for what they'd stood for, some version of a shared life that had been present and was now more complicated.

Naming anticipatory grief is the first step toward processing it. You can say: I miss what we had before. I'm afraid about what certain things will look like in the future. Neither of those statements requires her to fix anything. Both allow the grief to exist as information rather than pressure.

Compassion Fatigue

Compassion fatigue is the depletion that results from sustained empathic attention to another person's suffering. It was originally documented in professional caregivers, among nurses and trauma therapists, but the same process operates in informal partnerships where one person is providing ongoing support to someone in chronic pain or distress (Figley, 1995).

The signs are specific: reduced empathic capacity. Difficulty feeling moved by distress that previously moved you. A quality of numbness at the moments when you should feel most present. Physical exhaustion that doesn't correlate with activity level. A slow withdrawal from emotional engagement with the relationship.

Compassion fatigue doesn't mean you've stopped caring. It means the system that generates caring has been running without maintenance for too long. It's a physiological state, not a moral one. Recognizing it is the prerequisite for addressing it, and addressing it requires doing something differently, not trying harder at what you're already doing.

Gabriel reached compassion fatigue somewhere in year two and interpreted it as becoming a worse person. The numbness he felt during Zoe's harder flares, the inability to be moved by something that had genuinely moved him in year one, had felt like evidence of selfishness or deterioration. It was evidence of depletion. The distinction between those two things changes what you do next. Selfishness requires correction. Depletion requires replenishment.

The practical difference is significant. A partner who believes he's become selfish tries harder at the caring, which depletes him further. A partner who understands he's depleted looks for replenishment, which might mean therapy, or a week of building in genuine rest, or a conversation with Zoe in which he tells her the truth about how year two has felt. The first path spirals. The second path leads somewhere.

> **Action Step:** Writing Challenge: The Partner Emotional Audit Take fifteen minutes. Write down which of these five states is currently the loudest in your experience: guilt, resentment, grief, helplessness, or loneliness. Don't rank all five. Just identify the one that's most present right now. Then write three sentences about what's driving it. Then write one sentence about one specific thing that might reduce it. Keep this. Return to it in four weeks and note what's changed.

The "I Shouldn't Feel This" Trap

The single most consistent thing partners say when they finally describe their emotional experience is some version of: I know I shouldn't feel this way, because she's the one who's actually suffering. The logic is so uniform across partners that it qualifies as a pattern.

The logic is also flawed, and following it produces consistently bad outcomes. Its premise is: because her suffering is greater, mine doesn't count. But suffering isn't a competition with a fixed pool. Her pain doesn't cancel out your grief. The relationship contains two people, both of whom are being affected by a condition that only one of them has.

The "shouldn't feel this way" trap keeps partners from seeking support, from having the conversations that would actually help, from accessing the resources that would make them better partners. It keeps Gabriel in the car for twenty-two minutes when the thing he needs is to go inside and say to Zoe:

I'm not okay today. I've been keeping something from you and it's starting to cost more than it's worth.

When he finally said something close to that, Zoe's response was not what he'd feared. She'd been wondering for two years why he always seemed so even. She'd been interpreting his steadiness as distance: as evidence that the condition had made her feel like too much and him feel like he'd stopped needing her. The twenty-two minutes, when she heard about them, were a relief. They proved he was human. They proved the illness was affecting him too. She'd been carrying the belief that it wasn't, and that belief had been its own loneliness.

The "shouldn't feel this way" logic is so universal because it feels like virtue. It feels like putting her needs first. What it actually does is keep both partners isolated in parallel experiences that are never shared, which is worse for both of them. The research on dyadic coping says so clearly: couples who share their emotional experience, including the partner's emotional experience, fare better than those who manage separately.

What Actually Helps

Naming the emotion is the first move. Not in therapeutic vocabulary, not with clinical precision, but in plain language. I am angry. I am sad. I am running on empty in a way that sleep isn't touching. The act of naming moves an emotion from an undifferentiated physical state into something that can be examined and addressed.

Physical regulation comes before cognitive processing. The sustained activation of the stress response system has physiological consequences, and you can't examine what you're feeling when your nervous system is in a high-alert state. Walk before you talk. Exercise with genuine effort, not obligation. Get adequate sleep, not as an aspiration but as a genuine priority managed with the same attention as her medical appointments. These aren't platitudes. They're prerequisites.

Time-bounded containment: a strategy for partners who find that the emotions surface at inconvenient moments. Set a specific window, fifteen minutes daily or an hour weekly, in which you allow the feelings to be fully present without the obligation to also be functional. Outside that window, you're not suppressing. You're deferring. The nervous system responds differently to deferral than to suppression.

Telling someone who isn't your partner. Your partner is the person least positioned to support you regarding the impact of her illness. She has a direct conflict of interest. She may feel guilty. She may not have the capacity. Seeking her support for your feelings about the situation she's in creates a dynamic that is genuinely difficult to sustain. External support, from a therapist, a trusted friend who knows the full picture, a peer community, is what makes it possible to return to the relationship with something in reserve.

Building Your Own Support

Individual therapy is the most reliable structural support for the kind of processing this chapter describes. A therapist who understands chronic illness partnerships, or who is willing to learn the landscape, gives you a space where your experience is the primary subject rather than a secondary consideration. That space is genuinely rare in the rest of your life.

Gabriel started therapy in year three. He'd resisted it in years one and two on the grounds that his experience didn't warrant it: she was the one with the diagnosis, he was the well one, therapy was for people with real problems. He'd gone eventually because his GP had said, in a matter-of-fact way, that the symptoms he was describing, the fatigue and the numbness and the emotional flatness, were consistent with caregiver burnout, and that she was prescribing six sessions with a specific therapist as she would prescribe any other treatment.

He'd been reluctant. The therapy had been useful. The most useful thing wasn't a technique or a reframe. It was the therapist saying, in the third session, that everything he'd described was a reasonable response to a genuinely difficult situation, and that he didn't have to earn the right to find it hard. That sentence took about twenty minutes to properly land, and then it did, and something loosened.

In a Nutshell

The partner's emotional life in an endometriosis relationship includes guilt, resentment, anticipatory grief, and compassion fatigue in layered and overlapping forms. None are evidence of inadequate love. The guilt-resentment loop feeds itself and becomes more damaging the longer it runs without acknowledgment. Anticipatory grief is a real form of grief without a recognized social form, and naming it is the beginning of processing it. Compassion fatigue is a physiological depletion that requires a change in approach, not more effort. The "I shouldn't feel this" logic is consistently harmful and consistently wrong. Strategies that help include naming the emotion, physical regulation, time-bounded containment, and support from someone outside the relationship. Individual therapy and peer support are the most underused resources available to partners in this situation. Gabriel's twenty-two minutes in the car were the beginning of him understanding that he needed somewhere to put the feelings other than a parked car in the dark. This chapter is the beginning of building that somewhere.

Gabriel's twenty-two minutes became a kind of anchor for how he thought about his emotional life in the relationship. He'd return to the question sometimes: how full is the tank, honestly? Not fine. Actually. The question was useful because it forced him to answer before the depletion became the car, the list of four names, the numbness in year three. He'd learned to ask it earlier. That habit, small and private and practiced, was part of what kept the relationship intact.

Chapter 9: The Fertility Conversation -- Grief, Decisions, and Finding Your Way Forward

Marcel drove home from the fertility clinic without either of them saying much.

Ines was in the passenger seat looking out the window. He kept waiting for her to speak first because he didn't know which of the possible sentences wouldn't make things worse. He thought about saying: it was a lot of information. He thought about saying: we don't have to decide anything yet. He thought about reaching over and taking her hand.

He reached over and took her hand. She held it without turning from the window.

The consultation had lasted forty-five minutes. They'd been told about the endometrioma on Ines's left ovary and what it meant for her ovarian reserve on that side. They'd been given information about IVF, including a success-rate figure that was delivered carefully and was still frightening. Marcel had written things in a small notebook because writing was something to do with his hands, a way of being useful in a room where the only thing happening was the delivery of difficult information.

In the car he wanted to say something hopeful. He couldn't find the hope honestly. So he held her hand and drove and let the silence be what it needed to be. He thought: I have no idea how she's feeling. He thought: I have no idea how I'm feeling. Both of those thoughts were true, and neither of them helped.

The principle of this chapter: fertility grief in an endometriosis relationship is a dyadic experience. Both partners are grieving, often differently, often without acknowledging that the other is grieving too. The couple that navigates the fertility conversation without breaking doesn't have fewer feelings. They have better conversations about them, at the right moments, with the right honesty.

What the Statistics Mean

Endometriosis is common among people evaluated for infertility, and ESHRE notes that prevalence estimates may be as high as 50% in infertile women in some studies (ESHRE, 2022). The majority of women with endometriosis are able to conceive, either naturally or with medical support. Both of these things are true simultaneously and are frequently confused in both directions in online research.

The mechanisms by which endometriosis can affect fertility are multiple and distinct. Ovarian endometriomas, the cysts that endometriosis forms on or within the ovaries, reduce functional ovarian tissue and are associated with diminished ovarian reserve, which means fewer available eggs of potentially lower quality. Adhesions can compromise tubal function, affecting the egg's path toward the uterus. The inflammatory environment in the pelvis may create conditions that are less hospitable for implantation. Each mechanism is independent and they can co-occur.

What "endometriosis-associated infertility" means in practice varies significantly by individual. Some women with extensive endometriosis conceive without assistance. Some women with minimal disease face significant fertility challenges. The variability is one of the most frustrating features of counseling about this topic, because there is no reliable way to predict which situation applies without investigation. What the statistics provide is context; what the reproductive endocrinologist provides is the specific picture.

Data from the German IVF Register showed that approximately 11% of women undergoing IVF in Germany in 2020 carried an endometriosis diagnosis, making it one of the most common indications for assisted reproduction (German IVF Register, 2020). This statistic places endometriosis squarely within the mainstream of reproductive medicine, which is relevant context for couples entering that system for the first time.

Marcel had spent two evenings trying to understand what the population-level statistics meant for them specifically and had concluded that they didn't, exactly. What mattered was Ines's specific anatomy, her specific endometrioma, her specific reserve. The statistics were an orientation to the territory. They weren't a prediction about their particular journey.

The Partner's Grief Is Real

The partner's fertility grief in an endometriosis relationship is real, significant, and almost entirely unacknowledged in both clinical settings and in the relationships themselves.

In clinical settings, the fertility consultation is oriented toward the patient. The partner attends. He absorbs information. His emotional experience is rarely assessed, rarely addressed, and almost never asked about directly.

In the relationship, the same logic operates as elsewhere in the endometriosis experience: she's the one whose body is involved, her grief has priority, his can wait. The waiting accumulates.

Marcel had been grieving quietly for eight months before the fertility consultation. He'd been grieving a version of the future he'd imagined, with children in it, in a way that felt specific and concrete, not abstract or hypothetical. He'd been processing it privately, on the drive to work, in the half-hour before sleep, in the particular silence when friends announced pregnancies at dinner and he had to produce a face that didn't reveal what the announcement cost him. He hadn't told Ines any of this because he was afraid it would add to what she was already carrying.

Research on couples navigating infertility shows that infertility-related stress, coping patterns, and dyadic adjustment are associated with anxiety, depression, and relationship outcomes in both partners (Zurlo et al., 2020). When partners suppress their own distress to protect each other, the intention may be kind, but the practical effect can be isolation rather than support.

> **Teaching Point:** *The partner's fertility grief isn't smaller because he doesn't have the diagnosis. It's different grief with equal claims on acknowledgment. Couples who can name both griefs explicitly, and hold them together rather than sequentially, navigate this chapter of the relationship with significantly less relational damage.*

How Distress Becomes Shared

Research on couples navigating both chronic illness and fertility challenges has documented what researchers call dyadic effects: the process by which one partner's emotional state significantly shapes the other's, in both directions, often without either partner being aware it's happening.

When one partner's distress is high and unacknowledged, communication about the subject of distress tends to reduce. Both partners become careful around the topic. The carefulness looks like protection and functions like avoidance. The avoidance allows misreadings to accumulate. Ines, in the months before the consultation, had sometimes wondered whether Marcel was less affected by the fertility question than she was, because he seemed so steady. He was steady because he was protecting her from his feelings. She was reading his protection as indifference.

Couples who use dyadic coping--meaning they treat infertility-related stress as a shared problem rather than two private burdens--tend to report better quality of life and relationship adjustment than couples who manage distress in parallel (Zurlo et al., 2020; Zhao et al., 2024). The couples with better outcomes don't have fewer difficult feelings. They have more room to name the difficult feelings together.

> **Action Step:** Writing Challenge: The Fertility Conversation Starter Independently, without showing each other, each of you writes two things: your honest hopes around the fertility question right now, and your honest fears. Not your considered position on IVF or adoption or alternative futures. Your actual emotional reality this week. Then choose a low-pressure moment, not a difficult day and not immediately around a medical

> appointment, and share what you wrote. The goal of this exercise is not to reach a decision. It's to find out what the other person is actually carrying.

What IVF Actually Involves

Partners often arrive at the IVF conversation with a vague awareness that it exists as an option and limited understanding of what it requires of either of them.

In vitro fertilization involves hormonal stimulation of the ovaries to produce multiple eggs, egg retrieval under light sedation, fertilization of retrieved eggs in a laboratory, and transfer of one or more resulting embryos to the uterus. The stimulation phase requires frequent monitoring appointments, typically every one to two days. The hormonal medications involved can produce significant physical effects, including bloating, mood variability, and fatigue that may be pronounced.

Success rates depend on multiple factors, principally age and ovarian reserve. For women under 35 with a good reserve, live birth rates per cycle are in the range of 30 to 40%. For women with reduced ovarian reserve, including those whose reserve has been affected by endometriosis, rates may be lower. A reproductive endocrinologist who has assessed Ines's specific results is the right source for realistic expectations.

Your practical role in the IVF process: be present at consultations when she wants you there. If she needs help with self-administered injections, learn how to assist if she'd like that. Manage the household during the stimulation phase when she may have limited physical and emotional capacity. And have the conversation in advance about what you'll do together if a cycle fails.

The failure conversation before a first cycle feels premature. It isn't. Couples who have a shared understanding of how they'll handle a negative result before the result arrives are significantly more likely to remain cohesive when it does. The plan doesn't have to be elaborate. It can be as simple as: if this doesn't work, we take two weeks before making any decisions about the next step.

Marcel and Ines went through three IVF cycles over twenty months. The third was the one that worked. But before the third cycle, they had a conversation about what they would do if it was also the last. They cried. They told each other things about their hopes and fears that they'd been withholding for most of the fertility process. The conversation didn't make the third cycle succeed. It made them capable of being in the room together, intact, whatever happened.

Conversations About the Future

Not every couple pursuing endometriosis-related fertility treatment will have a biological child. Not every couple will pursue treatment. The conversations about what comes next, including childfree living, adoption, fostering, and other paths, are among the most consequential a couple can have and among the most avoided.

They're avoided because they feel like foreclosing. If we discuss adoption, does that mean we've given up? If we discuss being childfree, does that mean I've accepted something she hasn't? These concerns are understandable. They're also why many couples never have the conversation at all and arrive at major life decisions through exhaustion and default rather than through genuine shared deliberation.

What the conversation requires is a permission structure rather than a decision. Can we look together at what the future might look like if biological children aren't part of it? is a question that opens a space without closing any option. It doesn't mean you've decided. It means you're able to think about the full range of possible lives, which is a necessary capacity for navigating any of them.

Adoption, fostering, childfree living, and other alternatives are legitimate lives. Couples who arrive at those options via an honest shared process have better outcomes than those who arrive via avoidance and accumulation. The conversation is hard. Having it is what makes whichever outcome follows bearable.

The car ride home from that first consultation was the beginning of Marcel and Ines's fertility chapter. They said very little. He held her hand. That was the right thing to do on that particular day, and he knew it even without a script. But the conversations that came after, the ones they'd prepared for and had honestly, were what determined whether they remained together and whole through what followed. Silence is appropriate for car rides home from difficult appointments. It isn't a strategy for the months that come after.

Grieving the Family That May Not Happen

Some couples will reach a point of confirmed infertility, or a decision to stop pursuing pregnancy, and will need to grieve the biological family that isn't going to happen. This grief is real, significant, and has no culturally agreed-upon form. There's no funeral. No announced loss. The people around you may not know what you've been hoping for, and may not know they should be offering condolences.

The grief for a future that doesn't happen is different from the grief for something lost. It's grief for an absence, which is harder to name and harder to be acknowledged for. Marcel and Ines's friends knew they'd been through IVF. They didn't know the full weight of what three cycles had cost, emotionally and financially and relationally. When the third cycle worked, the relief was enormous. But Marcel has thought since about the couples they knew from the fertility support group, some of whom are still in that grief, and the absence of social infrastructure to hold it.

Frameworks that help with this kind of grief include narrative approaches: writing explicitly about what you'd imagined, what it felt like to hope for it, and what it means to let that version of the future go. They include dyadic grief, which means grieving together rather than in parallel, with honesty about what each person is mourning. And they include, where possible, redirection: the gradual investment in an alternative future that's genuinely chosen rather than settled for. This last one takes time and can't be forced. But it can be oriented toward.

The couple that navigates infertility grief together, in whatever form the grief takes, tends to emerge with a more explicit relationship than they had before. They've had to put things into words that most couples leave implicit. They've had to negotiate fundamental questions about what they want their lives to look like. That negotiation, hard as it is, produces something durable.

In a Nutshell

Endometriosis affects fertility through multiple documented mechanisms, including reduced ovarian reserve, tubal involvement, and altered implantation conditions. The partner's fertility grief is real, under-acknowledged in clinical settings and in the relationship itself, and produces worse outcomes when suppressed than when named. Dyadic suppression consistently produces worse outcomes than shared grief. IVF requires practical preparation and advance conversations about how to handle failure, before failure occurs. Conversations about the full range of future possibilities require a permission structure rather than a decision. The grief for a biological family that doesn't happen is a real grief without a social form, and frameworks for processing it include narrative work, dyadic grief, and the gradual investment in an alternative future that's genuinely chosen. The car ride home from the fertility clinic was Ines and Marcel's version of the corridor moment. What they built after it is the actual story.

Marcel kept the notes from the fertility consultation. Not because he needed to review them clinically, but because he'd written Ines's name and the date at the top of the page, and the act of keeping it felt like acknowledging that what happened in that room had happened, and that it mattered. Some things in an endometriosis partnership deserve to be witnessed rather than managed. The fertility chapter is one of them. Marcel and Ines had sat in a car afterward with very little to say. The words that mattered came later, in the weeks after, when they'd learned how to have the conversations this chapter describes. The car ride was appropriate. The silence was the right response to that particular moment. What followed the silence was the actual work.

Chapter 10: The Long Game -- Endometriosis as a Lifelong Companion

Oscar and Eloise were at a wedding, nine years in, and she was having a good day.

They were dancing. Not anything coordinated, just moving together the way people move at weddings when the mood is right and the evening has been good. She was laughing at something he'd said, and her dress was exactly the color she'd been trying to describe in the shop, somewhere between silver and blue, and she looked well.

He watched her and thought: we made it.

Then, almost immediately: we're not through it.

Both thoughts were true at the same time. That was what nine years looked like. You could be dancing at a wedding and she could be having a genuinely good day, you could mean it when you thought we made it, and you could also know clearly, without despair, that the condition hadn't gone anywhere. That next month's cycle would arrive and the management would resume and the long relationship between their life and this illness would continue. Two things, held simultaneously.

Oscar had learned to hold them. It had taken years. In year one, he'd believed you had to choose: either things were going to be okay or they weren't. The either-or was a crisis frame. By year nine he'd moved out of it, into something more durable. The principle of this chapter: endometriosis doesn't end. It is managed. What changes over years is the couple's capacity to hold that reality alongside everything else their life contains, without either letting the condition define the relationship or refusing to acknowledge its presence. That capacity is the long game.

The Chronic Illness Frame

One of the most useful shifts a partner can make, and one of the most difficult to make early in the experience, is the move from a crisis frame to a chronic illness frame.

The crisis frame treats each flare as a discrete emergency to be managed and survived. It positions endometriosis as a series of problems to be solved. It makes the good periods feel like the real life and the difficult ones feel like interruptions. The partner in the crisis frame is perpetually surprised by recurrence, perpetually hoping this is the last bad cycle, perpetually working against the condition rather than within a life that includes it.

The chronic illness frame understands that both the good periods and the difficult ones are the actual life. The condition is a continuous presence that recedes and returns rather than a set of individual events. This frame isn't more pessimistic than the crisis frame. It's more accurate, and accuracy produces better decisions over time.

Oscar had moved to the chronic illness frame somewhere around year five. He could identify the shift in retrospect because year five was when he stopped being surprised by bad months and started treating them as features of a familiar landscape rather than failures of management. The dread had been exhausting. The acceptance, which was not resignation but something more active, more like preparation, was more sustainable. He was no less sad about the bad months in year five than he'd been in year one. He was less blindsided by them, and that made an enormous difference to how he showed up during them.

The chronic illness frame also changes how the partner relates to recurrence before it happens. In the crisis frame, the partner between bad periods holds an implicit hope that the good period is permanent. When recurrence arrives, the hope is dashed, which generates both grief and a sense of being deceived. In the chronic illness frame, the good period is simply what the condition looks like right now, and the partner holds appropriate expectations. This isn't pessimism. It's the honest shape of the situation. The couples who find recurrence most destabilizing tend to be the ones who were most attached to the good period being the final state. The couples who absorb recurrence most steadily have been living inside the chronic illness frame throughout.

Recurrence and How to Respond

Recurrence after surgery is a feature of endometriosis, not a failure of either the patient or the surgical team. Even after excision, which has lower recurrence rates than ablation, symptoms return in a significant proportion of women over time. Understanding this before it happens means it doesn't constitute a relational crisis when it does.

Eloise's symptoms had returned approximately three years after her excision surgery. Oscar had been aware of it coming for about six weeks before she named it. He'd watched the pre-flare quality return to her stillness. He'd noticed the particular way she held herself in the days before a bad cycle. When she told him, he said: okay. Let's find out what the next step is.

He'd done the private grieving in the week before she said it. He'd felt genuine sadness about the return, about the renewed hope of the post-surgical period ending, about what the next management cycle would require of both of them. But he didn't grieve loudly in the conversation with her, because that conversation wasn't the right container for his grief. It was the container for hers, and for the practical planning that needed to happen.

Recurrence doesn't mean the excision surgery failed. It means the surgery did what it could do, which was reduce disease burden and extend the symptom-free or symptom-reduced period. That's what it was designed to do. The next step in management is a clinical question, approached with the same advocacy skills and clinical vocabulary covered in Chapter 6, in a new cycle.

The relational task around recurrence is to stay in the chronic illness frame rather than falling back into crisis mode. Oscar had practiced this. When Eloise told him, he didn't catastrophize about the future, didn't ask what this meant for everything they'd planned, didn't perform a grief that would have required her to manage his response alongside her own. He said: okay. Let's find out what the next step is. That sentence is the whole of the chronic illness frame in one line.

> **Action Step:** Writing Challenge: The State of Our Partnership Letter Write a letter to her. Not about endometriosis. About everything else. What you admire about who she is. What you are proud of in how you have both handled this together. What you are looking

> forward to. Something specific she's done or said recently that you want her to know you noticed. Give it to her this week. This letter is infrastructure, not sentiment. Do it whether things are going well or not.

The Emotional Phases of a Long Partnership

Long-term partnerships with chronic illness tend to move through identifiable phases, though the sequence isn't fixed and the phases can recur.

The early crisis phase covers the period of initial diagnosis and adjustment. High anxiety, high information demand, significant disruption to what the couple had understood their shared life to be. Both partners are learning the shape of the new situation.

The adaptation phase follows. The couple builds the habits and systems that make the condition navigable: the flare protocol, the appointment preparation routine, the shared understanding of what support she needs and when. This phase can last several years and produces a functional stability that looks, from outside, like the relationship has normalized.

The plateau phase is where long-term couples spend most of their time. The condition is present, it's managed, and life continues alongside it. The risk of the plateau is relational drift: the gradual erosion of connection that happens when the management of the condition becomes so automatic that the relationship's other dimensions get less deliberate attention. The couple that has been together for eight years may find, in the plateau, that what they talk about is mostly logistics, and that the parts of their relationship that have nothing to do with endometriosis have been quietly underinvested.

The recalibration phase follows recurrence, a significant treatment change, or any major shift in the clinical picture. It often feels like being returned to the early crisis phase, but couples who have been through the first cycle have tools they didn't have then. The recalibration tends to be shorter. Not easier, necessarily, but shorter.

Oscar and Eloise had been through the recalibration phase twice. The first time, when symptoms returned after surgery, was the hardest. The second time, five years later when a new management approach was needed, was genuinely hard but didn't feel like the end of anything. They'd built enough shared language by then, and enough shared history, that the recalibration had a different quality. It felt like returning to a set of skills rather than learning them for the first time. That's what the long game does over years: it turns the crisis competencies into background capability.

Protecting the Non-Illness Zones

The couples who report the highest relationship satisfaction over long-term endometriosis partnerships consistently describe maintaining areas of their shared life that are explicitly not organized around the condition.

Oscar and Eloise protected the quiz nights. That specific thing: a pub quiz at a specific place on a specific night, where the rule, stated early and maintained over years, was that they didn't talk about anything clinical unless it happened to be a quiz question. It sounds trivial. Over nine years, it was among the most important habits they kept. It was a zone in which they were simply two people who liked being somewhere together, and the illness was not in that zone.

The non-illness zone doesn't have to be an activity. It can be a conversation topic they always have at dinner on one particular night. It can be a shared hobby that exists entirely outside the management sphere. It can be the specific quality of a morning they've agreed to protect from any endometriosis-related discussion. The content matters less than the consistency. You're signaling, to each other, that the relationship contains more than the illness, and that the more is being actively maintained.

Oscar and Eloise also had a rule about the first ten minutes after either of them came home. No endometriosis discussion in the first ten minutes. Just them. It was a small rule and they broke it sometimes, when something was urgent. But they held it most of the time, and what it created was: every day began with at least ten minutes of being two people who liked each other and had things to say that weren't about a medical condition. Over nine years, that adds up to something real.

The non-illness zones need protecting partly because the illness doesn't protect them. Endometriosis is an invasive condition in every sense: it moves into physical space, relational space, calendar space, financial space, and if you're not deliberate about the zones that remain free from it, it fills those too. The deliberateness doesn't require effort commensurate with the zones' importance. It requires a decision, made once and honored with modest consistency: this area is ours. Not the illness's. Ours.

When the Relationship Shows Strain

Chronic illness partnerships have higher rates of relational difficulty than the general population. This is not a reason to expect failure. It's a reason to recognize the warning signs before they compound.

The warning signs are gradual: increasing emotional distance that both partners rationalize. Communication that's become primarily logistical. Resentment that surfaces more often than before and takes longer to resolve. A quality of polite coexistence where warmth used to be. A reduction in physical affection, even the non-sexual kind.

Couples therapy for chronic illness relationships is well evidenced, and significantly more effective when entered as maintenance than as emergency intervention. A couple who begins therapy in year two, when patterns are still being set, faces a different and shorter therapeutic task than a couple who begins in year six after years of accumulated unaddressed material. The resistance to adding another commitment to an already demanding situation is understandable. The case against the resistance is simple: the relationship is the container in which all of this is happening. If the container develops cracks, the management of everything else becomes harder. Investing in the container is part of the plan.

Advocacy Beyond the Relationship

March is Endometriosis Action Month. This annual awareness campaign, coordinated by endometriosis organizations internationally, creates moments where public conversation about the condition is more accessible than usual.

As someone who has lived inside an endometriosis relationship, you have a perspective that is different from the patient's perspective and from the general public's. You know what it looks like from the side of the bed, from the waiting room, from the corridor. That perspective has value in public conversations about a condition that affects 190 million people globally (WHO, 2025) and still gets dismissed regularly in clinical settings.

Engagement doesn't require a public platform. It can mean sharing accurate information when someone in your network dismisses the condition. It can mean supporting her in whatever advocacy role she chooses. It can mean contributing to the organizations whose research and policy work have built the infrastructure of endometriosis care that she, and you, have depended on.

When the Relationship Is at Serious Risk

There's a difference between the relational strain that's a normal feature of a chronic illness partnership and the relational erosion that requires urgent attention. Both are worth naming.

Normal strain: cycles of resentment and repair that follow flares or difficult periods and resolve. A period where communication is primarily logistical, followed by a return to fuller engagement. Occasional emotional distance that closes when addressed. These are features of any relationship under sustained pressure and don't require alarm.

Erosion: resentment that doesn't repair between episodes. A year or more where the relationship has felt primarily functional rather than connected. Physical distance, including the kind that isn't about her pain, that has become the norm. One or both partners privately wondering whether this is sustainable. These are signals that something requires attention before it compounds further.

The difference between the two is often a matter of degree and duration. Most partners can identify which category their current situation falls into if they're honest about it. The question isn't whether things are hard, because things are hard, it always has been, and that's expected. The question is whether the hard has been accumulating or resolving.

Oscar and Eloise went through a period in year six that was closer to erosion than strain. They recognized it because they'd been through strain before and knew what that looked like, and this felt different. They started couples therapy not because the relationship was in crisis but because the distance had been increasing for long enough to warrant deliberate intervention. The therapist they saw had experience with chronic illness relationships and spent the first session asking about what was still working, not only what wasn't. That framing, what's still intact, was useful. It gave them somewhere to build from.

In a Nutshell

The chronic illness frame, which understands endometriosis as a managed lifelong companion rather than a recurring crisis, is more accurate and more sustainable than the crisis frame over years. Recurrence after surgery is a clinical event with a management pathway, not a failure, and the response to it is the same set of advocacy and management skills developed in the first cycle. Long-term partnerships move through early crisis, adaptation, plateau, and recalibration phases, each with different relational demands. Non-illness zones in the shared life are infrastructure, not sentiment. Warning signs of relational strain are gradual and recognizable; the distinction between strain and erosion is partly a matter of duration and whether things are resolving or accumulating. Couples therapy works better as maintenance than as emergency. The two truths Oscar held on the wedding dancefloor, we made it and we're not through it, are not contradictions. They're the full and accurate picture of what a long endometriosis partnership actually looks like. Both are worth holding.

Chapter 11: Scripts, Conversations, and the Language of Support

Martin spent about fifteen minutes composing a message to Clara's mother on a Tuesday morning.

Clara's mother had called the previous evening and said, in the careful way she had of saying difficult things, that she worried Clara was using the endometriosis as a reason not to engage with life. She'd said it with genuine love rather than malice, which was almost worse, because it left Martin without a clear target for the frustration he felt. He wanted to correct her. He didn't want to create a conflict that Clara would eventually have to manage herself. He wanted to explain the condition clearly. He didn't know, exactly, which facts to lead with and which to leave out. He didn't know how long to make the message.

He typed and deleted three drafts. He closed the app and went to work. The conversation sat unresolved in the background of the week.

This chapter exists because Martin's Tuesday morning is every partner's Tuesday morning. The right words for the difficult conversations don't come naturally, not because the people having them are inarticulate, but because the situations are genuinely hard and the standard social scripts don't fit. These scripts are starting points. They're written in a general register that needs to be adapted to your own voice, your own relationship, and the specific person you're speaking to. The structure of each script is the part that matters: acknowledge before requesting, name what's already present before introducing what you want. Keep the structure and adapt the language.

Martin eventually sent a short message to Clara's mother. He used two sentences from this chapter and rewrote the rest in his own voice. He sent it. Clara's mother called two days later and said, in a different tone: I hadn't realized it was like that. That call was worth the fifteen minutes of typing and deleting. It changed what Clara's relationship with her mother looked like for the next year. Words at the right moment matter. The preparation is what makes them available.

The principle of this chapter: the right words don't require inspiration. They require preparation. Preparing in advance, at a moment of calm, is what makes you useful in the moments that don't allow for calm. This chapter is the preparation.

Explaining the Condition to Skeptical People

When someone says "it's just a bad period" or "she should push through it," they're not usually being malicious. They've absorbed the cultural normalization of menstrual pain that has allowed endometriosis to go under-diagnosed for generations. Your task is to give them enough accurate information to update their understanding without creating a conflict that Clara, or whoever you're protecting, will eventually have to manage.

For a family member: "I understand it can look like that from the outside. What the doctors have confirmed is that there is tissue growing in places it shouldn't be in her pelvis, and it bleeds and causes inflammation with each cycle. On the worst days, the pain is genuinely incapacitating. She isn't choosing to limit herself. Her body is limiting her, on those days."

For a colleague asking why she misses work: "She has a gynecological condition that causes severe cyclical pain. She's under specialist care and there are days each month where she genuinely can't work normally. I know it can seem inconsistent given that she seems well other days. The condition is episodic. That's how it works."

For "but she was fine last week": "The condition doesn't cause constant symptoms. Some days are manageable and some aren't. A good day doesn't mean the difficult days aren't real. It means the cycle is in a different phase.'"

You don't owe anyone a complete medical education in a single conversation. If they want more information, the Endometriosis UK website and the Endometriosis Foundation of America have accessible public resources you can point them to. You can give them a sentence and a link. You don't have to carry the explanation indefinitely.

The most useful long-term script for skeptical people in your regular life isn't a medical explanation. It's a social boundary: "She has a chronic condition that affects her differently on different days. On the difficult days, she's not choosing to limit herself." That sentence closes the conversation without inviting debate. Most people who hear it will accept it. The ones who don't aren't going to be persuaded by clinical detail anyway, and you don't have to persuade them. You have to state the fact and move on.

Flare-Day Language

The scripts for flare-day communication are the most used in this chapter because flares happen regularly and the improvised response tends to be the harmful one, for the reasons covered in Chapter 4.

When she's in pain and you arrive: "I can see you're hurting. I'm here. Tell me what would help if there's anything, and if there isn't, I'll just be nearby."

If she isn't speaking: sit close enough that she knows you're there. Don't require a response. "I'm going to sit with you for a bit. You don't have to say anything."

If she needs practical help and hasn't asked: "I'm going to [handle this specific thing]. I'll check back in an hour." Give her information she doesn't have to request. Reduce decisions.

What not to say: "Is it really that bad?" "Can you rate the pain?" "I just don't know how to help." "Maybe you should try [unsolicited remedy]." "This always happens when we have plans." Each of these adds a burden to an experience that has already exceeded her capacity.

When she tells you to go away: "Okay. I'll be in the next room. The heat pad is by the door if you want it." Then go. Check in by text rather than by reappearing. The check-in is: "How are you doing? Anything you need?" Not: "Are you feeling better yet?"

Clinic Appointment Scripts

These scripts build on the framework in Chapter 6 and are consolidated here as a practical reference.

Introducing yourself: "I'm Clara's partner. She's asked me to be here to help take notes and support the conversation."

When "let's wait and see" is the response: "We've been managing this for [duration] and the symptoms have been [progressive/unchanged/worsening]. What specific outcome would change the recommendation toward more active investigation? Can you give us a threshold so we know what to watch for?"

Requesting specialist referral: "Could you refer her to a centre with specialist expertise in endometriosis management? We'd like access to a surgeon who operates on this condition regularly."

After a dismissal: "I want to make sure I've understood correctly. The recommendation is continued monitoring rather than further investigation. I'd like to have that noted in today's clinical record."

Requesting second opinion: "We'd like to seek a second opinion from an endometriosis specialist. Could you provide a referral, or recommend a centre?"

When she can't advocate: ask her permission first. "Would it help if I take the lead on the questions today?" Then proceed if she agrees.

A note on delivery: these scripts are written in formal English. In a real consultation, the language adapts to the register of the room. If the consultant is informal, you can be informal. If she's clinical and precise, match that. The content of the script, the specific request, the specific threshold, the specific record notation, is what matters. The exact words are negotiable. The underlying clarity of purpose is not.

The clinic script Martin had wished he had, for that first appointment where Clara was dismissed, was something like:

"We've been seeing multiple clinicians over two years and the symptom pattern hasn't changed. Can you tell us what would need to be different for a more thorough investigation to be warranted?" That question puts the burden of proof back on the clinical decision rather than on Clara's description of her pain. It changes the structure of the conversation. It's the kind of question that becomes easy to ask once you know it's possible, and impossible to formulate when you're sitting in the room without preparation.

Intimacy and Fertility Conversation Openers

These scripts assume you've identified a calm, low-pressure moment: not during or after a flare, not immediately following a difficult appointment, not when either person is depleted.

Opening the intimacy conversation: "I've been missing being physically close to you, and I've noticed that I've been pulling back too, partly because I didn't want to put pressure on you. I'd like us to be able to talk about it."

If she seems reluctant: "You don't have to respond to this right now. I just wanted to say it so it wasn't sitting between us without a name."

If she asks what you want: "I want us to be physically close in whatever way is comfortable for you. I don't need penetrative sex to be the definition of our physical life if it isn't possible right now. I want more connection than we've been having, and I'm open to what that looks like."

Opening the fertility conversation: "I've been thinking about [this question / what our future looks like]. Can we find time to talk about it? Not to make any decisions. I just want to know what you're thinking."

Sharing your own position in the fertility conversation: "I want to be honest with you about where I am emotionally. Not to burden you, but because I think you deserve to know. I've been [grieving / scared / uncertain] and I haven't said it."

Expressing Your Own Needs

This is the set of scripts most partners are most reluctant to use. They're included because the avoidance of expressing needs is one of the most consistent drivers of partner depletion, for the reasons covered in Chapter 8.

Naming depletion: "I want to be honest with you. I've been running low for a while, and I haven't said anything because I didn't want to add to what you're managing. I think I need [specific thing: time, a conversation, some support from you]."

After a difficult flare: "I'm glad you're feeling a bit better. When you have some capacity, I'd like to tell you how this week has been for me. Not to complain. I just don't want to keep editing myself."

Requesting space: "I need a few hours to myself today. Not because anything is wrong between us. I just need to refill."

Asking for reciprocity: "I know this is hard for you and I don't want to minimize that. I also want to be able to talk about what I'm carrying sometimes. I'd like us to find a way to hold both."

The script for expressing your own needs is the one most partners never try in its direct form. They soften it, qualify it, lead with so many acknowledgments that the actual request disappears inside the preamble. The structure that works is: state what you need, state why it matters, leave space for her to respond. The preamble is permitted. Three sentences of preamble is the maximum before the request gets lost. One sentence and a clear request is better.

Gabriel had practiced saying "I'm not okay today" for about a month before he said it to Zoe. He'd said it to his therapist first, then to himself on runs. The first time he said it to Zoe, she looked at him and said: finally. She'd been waiting two years for him to say something like that.

> **Action Step:** Behavior Challenge: Identify the one conversation you've been avoiding. Find the relevant section in this chapter. Read the script once silently. Then read it aloud, alone, to hear how the words sound in your voice rather than on the page. Then rewrite two or three sentences in your own phrasing. Practice the adapted version once more. You don't need to be word-perfect. You need to be ready enough to begin.

A Clinical Reference Glossary

The following terms appear in clinic settings and in this book. Having them in one place makes the reference chapter complete.

ASRM staging: American Society for Reproductive Medicine classification of endometriosis in four stages by extent and adhesion severity. Stage does not predict pain severity.

ESHRE: European Society of Human Reproduction and Embryology. Their 2022 guideline on endometriosis is the authoritative clinical reference document for best-practice management.

Adenomyosis: endometrial-type tissue within the uterine muscle wall. Often co-presents with endometriosis. Causes heavy periods and pelvic pain.

Pelvic floor dysfunction: chronic hypertonicity of the pelvic floor muscles, contributing to dyspareunia and other pelvic symptoms. Treated by specialist physiotherapy.

Excision: surgical removal of endometriotic lesions in their entirety, including the root. Preferred over ablation per ESHRE 2022 guidelines.

Ablation: destruction of the surface of endometriotic lesions using heat, laser, or electrical current. Does not remove the full depth of the lesion.

BSGE: British Society for Gynaecological Endoscopy. Maintains a list of accredited endometriosis centres in the UK.

AAGL: American Association of Gynecologic Laparoscopists. Lists members with specific interest in endometriosis management.

Nancy's Nook: a patient-community resource on Facebook that maintains a widely used crowd-sourced list of experienced excision surgeons, particularly useful in countries where specialist finder tools are less comprehensive.

The purpose of this glossary isn't to make you fluent in clinical language. It's to make sure that when a consultant uses one of these terms, you can follow the sentence rather than falling out of the conversation. The partner who knows these terms doesn't need to consult a phone during an appointment.

The partner who doesn't know them will always be slightly behind.

Scripts for "You Seem Fine" and "Just a Bad Period"

These responses come from family, friends, colleagues, and sometimes from your own head. They need a short, calm, complete sentence in response.

When someone says "she always seems fine when I see her": "The condition is episodic. The difficult days don't always coincide with social occasions, and she's very practiced at managing in social settings. That doesn't mean the difficult days aren't real."

When someone says "everyone has period pain": "This is a surgical diagnosis. The tissue is in places it shouldn't be. The pain isn't equivalent to normal menstrual discomfort."

When the response is your own internal voice: "The fact that she had a good day yesterday doesn't mean today's pain isn't real. The condition is episodic. I know this." State it to yourself plainly. The self-directed version matters as much as the external one.

In a Nutshell

The right words for hard conversations don't come naturally. They come from preparation at a calm moment. This chapter provides starting-point scripts for explaining the condition to skeptical people, communicating during a flare, navigating clinical appointments, opening the intimacy and fertility conversations, expressing your own needs, and responding to the "you seem fine" dismissal. The structure of each script is consistent: acknowledge before requesting, name what's present before introducing what you want. These scripts need to be adapted into your own voice. The goal is the conversation itself, not a perfect performance of the script. Martin had fifteen minutes of typing and deleting on a Tuesday morning. The scripts in this chapter are what those fifteen minutes needed.

Chapter 12: Building Your Support Ecosystem

Sometime in year three, Gabriel made a list.

He didn't plan to. He was on a delayed train with a pen and some paper and he started writing names. Who could he call if he needed to talk. Properly talk, not the version of talking where he was fine and managed and had made his adjustments. The version where he said: I am not okay today.

He counted the names. Then counted them again.

Four. He had four people he could call, and only one of them knew the full picture of what his life looked like from the inside. He had a brother who lived in another city and who he spoke to once a month about things that weren't this. He had colleagues he liked but didn't confide in. He had friends from before, from the years when plans were easier, some of whom had stopped asking how Zoe was because they didn't know how to respond when the answer was complicated.

He'd been keeping the full picture to himself because telling people felt like a betrayal of Zoe's privacy, or like complaining about something she was suffering more than he was, or like admitting to a weakness he should have managed. All of those reasons were understandable. All of them were costing him something he hadn't noticed losing until he sat on a delayed train counting names.

The principle of this chapter: partners of people with chronic conditions need their own support structures. This isn't selfish. It's sustainable. The caregiver literature is consistent that informal caregivers show worse psychological and physical health than non-caregivers, especially when caregiving stress is high and support is limited (Pinquart & Sörensen, 2003). The support isn't a distraction from the caregiving role. It's what makes the caregiving role viable across years.

Why Partners Need Support

The argument that your needs are secondary to hers in this situation rests on logic that is both understandable and incorrect.

It's understandable because she has the diagnosis, the pain, and the medical management. The scale of what she carries is real. But the argument isn't about relative need. It's about system function. You are a component of a system that requires maintenance to keep working. If you run that component without maintenance long enough, it degrades. The degradation doesn't only affect you. It affects the quality of support she receives from you, the quality of the relationship, and her own health outcomes, which research shows are associated with the quality of her support network.

The literature on informal caregiver burden is extensive and consistent. Informal caregivers show higher stress and depression and poorer subjective wellbeing and physical health than non-caregiving populations (Pinquart & Sörensen, 2003). These outcomes are not inevitable. They're the predictable risk of sustained caregiving without adequate personal support, and adequate support can reduce that risk.

Gabriel had been running depleted for three years. When he made the list on the train, he did something about it. The changes were incremental. He told his brother more about what their life actually looked like. He found a therapist. He started running, badly at first and then adequately. He joined an online partner forum and lurked for six weeks before he posted anything. Each change was small. The cumulative effect was significant.

The four names on the list became seven by the end of year four. Not because he'd worked at it intensively, but because each small step had opened the next one. He'd told his brother more, and his brother had started calling differently. He'd been honest in therapy, and that honesty had made it easier to be honest elsewhere. The list was a diagnostic tool. What it showed him was that the support ecosystem needed building, not pruning.

Finding Peer Support

Peer support from other partners of people with endometriosis provides something that professional support doesn't entirely replicate: the recognition of shared specific experience. The quality of understanding that comes when someone else has sat in the same hospital car park, sent the same kind of message to the same kind of skeptical family member, and felt the same guilt about the same feelings is a resource that happens to be free and available.

Endometriosis UK has partner-specific information and some community resources. The ENDOPART study, a qualitative research project examining the experiences of partners of women with endometriosis, has produced findings that many partners describe as the first time they've seen their own experience described accurately in a professional context. The Endometriosis Foundation of America and similar organizations maintain online communities that include partner participation.

Online communities vary in quality and activity level. The useful ones are where real people describe real situations with appropriate specificity. Lurk before you engage. The engagement builds over time, and the specific recognition that comes from reading someone describe your own experience in their own words is genuinely useful in a way that's distinct from the usefulness of therapy.

> **Action Step:** Behavior Challenge: The Support Ecosystem Map Take a piece of paper and draw a circle with four quadrants. Label them: emotional, practical, social, professional. In each quadrant, write one resource you currently have and one you currently lack. Emotional might be a therapist, a friend who knows the full picture, or a peer community. Practical might be someone who can cover household responsibilities during a bad week. Social might be any friend whose company doesn't require performance. Professional might be a GP or therapist with experience of chronic illness. Look at the gaps. Pick one. Make one specific move toward filling it this week, not this month.

Couples Therapy as Maintenance

There is a persistent assumption that couples therapy is for relationships in trouble. This assumption does consistent damage, because it means couples wait until the relationship is in significant difficulty before accessing the most effective relational intervention available.

Couples therapy for chronic illness partnerships, entered before significant damage has accumulated, functions as maintenance rather than repair. A couple who meets with a therapist for eight to twelve sessions in year two of an endometriosis relationship, when the adjustment is happening and the patterns are being established, has a very different and shorter therapeutic task than a couple who enters in year six after years of accumulated resentment, suppressed grief, and distance.

The specific focus that's most useful in couples therapy for endometriosis relationships covers what gets said and what gets withheld, the distribution of household and emotional labor, the partner's processing of their own emotional experience, and the patterns that have developed around intimacy. A therapist with chronic illness experience can work across all of these.

Gabriel and Zoe started couples therapy in year three. They'd entered it following a specific argument that had revealed the scale of what had been accumulating. The therapist had said, in their second session, that the argument was a useful indicator but not the problem. The problem was three years of two people managing parallel to each other rather than together. The subsequent year of work changed the relationship in ways Gabriel hadn't expected, not by resolving the illness, which it didn't, but by changing how they were together inside it.

Maintaining Friendships and Social Life

Chronic illness has a centrifugal effect on social life. Flare unpredictability makes committing to plans difficult. Repeated cancellations erode friendships. The management of social situations that require explanation creates fatigue that reduces motivation for the next one. Over years, couples can become increasingly isolated, which has documented negative effects on both physical and psychological health for both partners.

The specific challenge for the partner is that social isolation compounds the support deficit. Gabriel, by year three, had a list of four names. The social network that should have buffered the caregiving stress had quietly contracted while he wasn't watching it.

Strategies that help: flexible social arrangements where last-minute cancellations are genuinely fine without requiring explanation. Friends who know enough about the condition that explanation isn't required every time. Activities that don't depend on fixed attendance or schedule. The goal isn't a full social calendar alongside an endometriosis management calendar. It's a handful of relationships sustained honestly enough to function as support when you need them.

One specific strategy that partners of people with endometriosis report as useful is telling one or two close friends the full picture. Not the public version, not the polite version, but the actual experience, what the bad months look like, what the management involves, what it costs. Most people who are told the full picture respond with more authentic support than they'd been able to offer when they only had a partial one. The version of you that people in your life see is the composed version, the reliable version. The full picture version is also worth knowing, by someone who isn't Zoe.

Gabriel had told his brother the full picture in year three. His brother had gone quiet for a moment and then said: I didn't realize. I thought things were mostly okay because you seemed mostly okay. The distinction between seeming okay and being okay is the one most caregiving partners have been living inside for years. Saying it out loud, to someone who matters, changes something. The isolation doesn't require grand social reorganization. It requires honest speech to one or two people who are already in your life.

Setting Limits That Are Actually Healthy

Setting limits in a chronic illness relationship looks different from most other contexts, because the person whose needs you're navigating is someone you love who is genuinely unwell. The usual clean logic of limit-setting doesn't always apply.

Nevertheless, partners who set no limits tend to reach depletion at which the limits assert themselves involuntarily, in ways that are more damaging than intentionally set limits would have been. The choice isn't whether limits will be set. It's whether they're set deliberately or by breakdown.

There's a useful distinction between limits that protect your capacity, which are healthy and necessary, and limits that protect your comfort at her expense, which are a different matter. "I need three hours a week that are entirely mine" is the first kind. "I can't handle the medical appointments anymore" without offering an alternative is the second.

Healthy limit-setting in this context sounds like: "I want to be there for you in every way I can. I'm also noticing that I'm running low, and I need [specific thing]. Can we figure out together how to make that work?" The request is specific. It's framed as a shared problem. It leaves her space to respond.

The limits that are most worth setting are the ones that protect the practices that sustain you. The running. The therapy appointment. The time with a friend who knows the full picture. The morning window before anything gets discussed. These aren't luxuries. They're the maintenance that makes the caregiving possible across years rather than just months. Gabriel, once he'd started protecting them, found that their presence in the week was one of the clearest indicators of how he was actually doing. When the practices slipped, everything else started slipping too. When they held, everything held better.

Secondary Traumatic Stress

Secondary traumatic stress describes the psychological impact of sustained exposure to another person's trauma and suffering. It was first developed in work on professional and trauma-exposed caregivers; applying the concept to informal partnerships with chronic painful illness is a clinically useful analogy, but the endometriosis-specific evidence base is limited (Figley, 1995).

In a caregiving partner, it can look like this: intrusive thoughts about her pain episodes that surface at neutral moments. Hypervigilance about pre-flare indicators, a constant background monitoring of her signals that can't be switched off. A numbness at moments that should feel connecting. Avoidance of specific situations associated with past bad flares. A low-level ongoing anxiety that doesn't respond to reassurance because it isn't about a specific threat. It's about the pattern.

Gabriel had recognized the hypervigilance in himself by year three. He'd become very good at reading Zoe's micro-signals: the specific stillness before a bad flare, the way she held her lower abdomen, the particular quality of her going quiet.

He'd become so attuned to it that he couldn't fully switch the monitoring off, which meant he was never entirely at rest even on the good days. The running helped with this. The therapy helped more. Naming it as secondary traumatic stress rather than as a personality flaw helped most of all.

The naming matters for the same reason that naming any emotional experience matters: it moves the experience from an undifferentiated physical state into something that can be understood and addressed. "I'm a hypervigilant, depleted mess who has been running on fumes for two years" is a clinical description with a pathway. "I'm becoming a worse person" is a moral judgment with no pathway. The first has a response. The second only has a spiral.

The strategies that address secondary traumatic stress overlap significantly with the broader support strategies in this chapter. Physical regulation through consistent exercise. The therapy appointment held weekly, not cancelled when inconvenient. The peer connection that provides recognition rather than advice. The deliberate deactivation of the monitoring during non-illness zones of the shared life. None of these removes the hypervigilance entirely, any more than any other treatment removes the underlying condition entirely. But each one reduces the weight of it, and the cumulative reduction is significant.

In a Nutshell

Partners of people with endometriosis need their own support structures: emotional, practical, social, and professional. This isn't selfish; it's sustainable, and the research on caregiver outcomes is consistent on this point. Peer support from others who share the specific experience provides recognition that professional support doesn't fully replicate. Couples therapy works best as maintenance, entered early, before significant damage requires repair. Social isolation compounds the support deficit over years, and deliberately maintained flexible friendships are the countermeasure. Telling one or two people the full picture rather than the composed version changes both the relationship and the support you receive from it. Limits that protect capacity are healthy and necessary; they will be set eventually, either deliberately or by depletion. Secondary traumatic stress is a recognized consequence of sustained proximity to a partner's suffering, and it responds to the same strategies as other forms of caregiver burden. Gabriel had four names on his list when he sat on the delayed train in year three. By year four, he had seven. Not because he'd worked intensively at building the list, but because each honest step had opened the next one. Every caregiving partner who has been running depleted without naming it deserves what Gabriel eventually found: a space where the full picture is the one that's allowed. The list is worth building. Start with one name.

Conclusion: Becoming the Partner She Needs -- and the Person You Need to Be

Oscar had kept the paragraph.

He'd written it on the night after the corridor, when Eloise had gone to bed early and he'd sat at the kitchen table with his phone and typed into a notes app. He'd titled it "what the hardest part is so far" and put it away and not looked at it for months.

Nine years later he found it, by accident, while looking for something else. He read it.

He'd written: The hardest part is standing next to her and having nothing to offer. I don't know what's happening in her body. I don't know what to say. I don't know when to speak and when to be quiet and when to just leave the room. She's in pain and I'm useless and I can't figure out how to be less useless, and I'm frightened about what this means for the rest of our lives.

He read it a second time. He remembered the kitchen table, the cold coffee, the printout folded on the counter. He sat with it for a few minutes.

Then he wrote something new.

He wrote: The hardest part now is different. It's the days when she has pain I can't take away, even though I know what it is and what's causing it and what to do. It's the recalibration after recurrence, which I've done twice now and still don't find easy. It's the maintenance, staying present and invested across years when the condition doesn't go away and the management doesn't stop. But I know what I'm doing. I know the biology, the surgical landscape, the clinical vocabulary. I know how to sit on the bathroom floor at 2 AM and be the right kind of present. I know how to walk into an appointment and change what happens in the room. I know the difference between being a problem-solver in a moment that needs a witness. I didn't know any of that the night I wrote the first paragraph. I know all of it now.

That shift, from the first paragraph to the second, is what this book has been trying to build.

What You Carry Now

Look at what you've covered in these chapters.

You understand the biology. You know what endometriosis is, why diagnosis took as long as it did, and why the delay wasn't a failure of the person you love but of a system with documented and recurring inadequacies. You know what happens in her body during a flare, and you know that the pain is physiologically appropriate to what's occurring, not a measure of weakness or exaggeration.

You have the clinical vocabulary. You know the difference between ablation and excision, and why it matters. You know what pelvic floor hypertonicity is and why it contributes to dyspareunia independently of surgical disease. You know what ESHRE says, and what BSGE accreditation means, and how to walk into a room and ask a question that changes what happens.

You have the emotional framework. You know the guilt-resentment loop and how to exit it. You know what anticipatory grief is and why it hasn't been named for you anywhere else. You know what compassion fatigue feels like in your own body and what it requires. You know that your emotional experience is real and has claims on acknowledgment, and that suppressing it doesn't protect her. It just delays the cost.

You have the practical tools. The flare protocol. The appointment scripts. The Sensate Focus framework. The conversation openers for the topics you've been avoiding. The Support Ecosystem Map with its four quadrants and its honest gaps.

The Shift from Helplessness to Agency

The reader who opened this book was, in most cases, the person in the corridor with nothing. No map, no language, no framework. Standing next to someone in pain and having no idea how to be useful.

That's not who you are at the end of it.

The shift from helplessness to agency in this context doesn't mean you've solved anything. It means you understand the landscape. It means you have words for the situations that previously left you speechless. It means the 2 AM bathroom floor is no longer a place of panic but a place of practice, where you know to sit down and say nothing and stay.

Oscar on the wedding dancefloor, nine years in, holding both truths at once: we made it, and we're not through it. That's what agency in this situation looks like. Not certainty. Not resolution. The capacity to hold the complexity without requiring it to resolve.

Endometriosis as a We-Disease

There's a frame that some researchers and advocates have applied to endometriosis in partnerships: the idea that the condition affects both partners and should be understood as a shared experience rather than one person's medical situation.

Not because your experience is equivalent to hers. It isn't. She has the pain, the diagnosis, the surgery, the medical management, the years of being told she was wrong about her own body. Her experience is primary.

But the research on endometriosis partnerships is consistent that the condition reshapes the lives of both people. It reshapes the financial landscape. The relational landscape. The physical intimacy landscape. The fertility landscape. The social and professional landscape. It affects both partners' psychological health. It creates a shared caregiving and management role that, when done well, requires both people.

Calling it a we-disease isn't about claiming equivalence. It's about claiming participation. Your presence in her clinical care, her flare management, her fertility decisions, her long-term wellbeing, is part of what determines the outcome. The research says so. This book has been built on that evidence. Your engagement matters. The fact that you're at the end of this book rather than the person in the corridor with nothing means you've chosen to matter in a specific, grounded, informed way.

What Sustained Partnership Actually Looks Like

It's imperfect. That's the first thing to say about it.

It's imperfect because you're human and the condition is chronic and there will be bad months that test the protocol you've built. There will be conversations that start with the right script and go sideways. There will be clinic appointments where you sit in the chair and forget the question you'd prepared. There will be evenings when the compassion fatigue is louder than the care, and you'll get back in the car for fifteen minutes before you can go inside. All of that is part of the actual picture.

The couples who sustain long-term endometriosis partnerships aren't the ones who never struggle. They're the ones who have the infrastructure to recover when they do. The flare protocol they return to. The conversation they've learned to have. The therapist who knows the landscape. The peer who has been in the same place. The non-illness zones they protect. The letter they wrote on a good day that sits in a notes app for nine years and proves, when found, that they were always trying.

The Final Action Step

There's one thing left to do.

Go back to what you wrote at the end of the introduction. The paragraph about the hardest part. Read it.

Then write a new paragraph. What's the hardest part now? It may be the same thing. It may be something different. It may be smaller than it was. It may have moved somewhere you didn't expect.

Then write a third paragraph: what do you have now that you didn't have before? Name the specific things. The clinical understanding. The vocabulary. The scripts. The emotional framework. The recognition that your experience is real and counts. The knowledge that sitting on a bathroom floor in the dark, saying nothing, staying, is one of the most useful things a partner can do.

Keep all three paragraphs together. They are the arc. They are the evidence.

You came in as the person in the corridor.

You leave as something better equipped. Not perfect. Not finished. Better equipped, and still trying.

That's what the long game requires. That's what it looks like when it works.

Appendix A: Clinical Reference Guide

ASRM Staging Summary

The American Society for Reproductive Medicine classifies endometriosis in four stages based on the extent and location of lesions and the severity of adhesions.

Stage 1 (Minimal): Isolated implants, no significant adhesions. Stage 2 (Mild): More superficial implants, minimal adhesions. Stage 3 (Moderate): Multiple superficial and deep implants, filmy adhesions, possible endometriomas. Stage 4 (Severe): Multiple deep implants, extensive adhesions, large endometriomas, possible bowel or bladder involvement.

Important: stage does not predict pain severity. A Stage 1 diagnosis can involve debilitating pain; a Stage 4 diagnosis can involve moderate symptoms. Pain is driven by lesion location, nerve involvement, and pelvic floor adaptation, not by stage alone.

Glossary of Key Terms

Adenomyosis: a condition where endometrial-type tissue grows within the uterine muscle wall. Often co-presents with endometriosis. Causes heavy, painful periods and an enlarged, tender uterus.

Ablation: surgical destruction of endometriotic lesions by burning their surface. Does not remove the full depth of the lesion. Associated with higher recurrence rates than excision.

Dyspareunia: pain during or after sexual intercourse. In endometriosis, caused by lesions in the pouch of Douglas, pelvic floor hypertonicity, and neurological sensitization.

Endometrioma: an ovarian cyst formed by endometriosis. Also called a "chocolate cyst." Can reduce ovarian reserve and is visible on pelvic ultrasound.

ESHRE: European Society of Human Reproduction and Embryology. Issues the authoritative clinical guidelines for endometriosis management. Current version published 2022.

Excision: surgical removal of endometriotic lesions in their entirety, including the root tissue. Preferred approach per ESHRE 2022 guidelines. Requires specialized surgical training.

Laparoscopy: minimally invasive surgical procedure using a camera and instruments inserted through small abdominal incisions. The only definitive diagnostic method for endometriosis. Treatment can be combined with diagnosis.

Pelvic floor dysfunction: chronic hypertonicity of the pelvic floor muscles. Contributes to dyspareunia, bowel and bladder symptoms, and persistent pelvic pain. Treated by specialist pelvic floor physiotherapy.

Pouch of Douglas: the space between the uterus and the rectum. A common site for deep endometriosis. Involvement in this area is a major cause of dyspareunia.

Current ESHRE Guideline Summary (2022)

The 2022 ESHRE guideline on endometriosis is the primary international clinical reference for management. Key recommendations relevant to partners include: surgical excision is preferred over ablation for endometriotic lesions where technically feasible; specialist centres with multidisciplinary teams should be the standard of care for complex or recurrent disease; pelvic floor physiotherapy is recommended for dyspareunia; and fertility should be discussed at diagnosis for all patients of reproductive age. The full guideline is available at https://www.eshre.eu/Guidelines-and-Legal/Guidelines/Endometriosis-guideline

Specialist Organizations by Region

United Kingdom: Endometriosis UK (www.endometriosis-uk.org). Provides patient and partner resources, a specialist centre finder via the BSGE-accredited centre list, and support group information.

United States: Endometriosis Foundation of America (www.endofound.org). Provides patient education, specialist referral resources, and awareness campaign materials.

International: European Society of Human Reproduction and Embryology (www.eshre.eu) for clinical guidelines. Nancy's Nook Endometriosis Education, a Facebook community (patient-facing but partner-inclusive), maintains a widely used crowd-sourced list of experienced excision surgeons.

Appendix B: Flare Response Card Template

The Flare Response Card is a two-sided reference document built together during a pain-free period. It should be reviewed and updated at least once a year or after any significant change in her clinical management.

Side One: Her Flare Profile

Her top three flare triggers, in order of reliability: [space for three entries].

Her preferred relief strategies, in order of what works best: [space for three entries, e.g., heat to lower abdomen, specific medication and dose, warm bath].

Her communication preference during a flare: [space for preference, e.g., silent company / space and check-ins by text / active conversation].

What she finds most helpful that partners often don't do: [free text].

What she finds least helpful that partners often do: [free text].

Side Two: The Escalation Threshold and Your Commitment

The signs that this flare warrants contacting a healthcare provider: [space for specific threshold, established with her medical team, e.g., pain significantly worse than her baseline and not responding to usual management; fever; inability to keep fluids down; any symptom she describes as different in character from her usual pattern].

Healthcare provider contact number for non-emergency escalation: [space].

Emergency contact if she cannot contact herself: [space].

Your commitment statement: I will be present without an agenda. I will not minimize, clock-watch, or offer unsolicited advice. I will stay until you ask me to go, and I will go when you ask. I am prepared for this, and I am here.

Appendix C: Partner Resources and Communities

Organizations

Endometriosis UK (www.endometriosis-uk.org): the UK's primary endometriosis charity. Partner resources are available under the "For Partners" section of the website. The BSGE-accredited specialist centre finder is at www.bsge.org.uk/centre.

Endometriosis Foundation of America (www.endofound.org): US-based organization with patient education resources and a specialist referral network.

ESHRE Endometriosis Guideline (www.eshre.eu): the 2022 clinical guideline is publicly accessible and written in plain language alongside the technical document.

Research Resources

The ENDOPART Study: a qualitative research project on the experiences of male partners of women with endometriosis. Findings have been published in peer-reviewed journals and are accessible via PubMed search for "ENDOPART endometriosis partners."

EndoVie Survey (published 2024): a French partner survey on the lived experience of partners of women with endometriosis, published in the European Journal of Obstetrics & Gynecology and Reproductive Biology.

Recommended Reading for Partners of Chronically Ill People

The Caregiving Wife's Handbook by Diana Denholm (2012): addresses the specific challenges of spousal caregiving across chronic illness, not endometriosis-specific but highly applicable.

How to Be Sick by Toni Bernhard (2010): written by a person with chronic illness, provides partners with deep perspective on what chronic illness management feels like from inside the experience.

Appendix D: Recommended Conversation Guides

The Clinic Preparation Template

Complete before any specialist appointment. Bring two copies.

Current symptoms with timing and severity (cyclical vs. constant, duration, rating on a scale used consistently): [space].

Current medications, dosages, and effects noted: [space].

Previous treatments tried and outcomes: [space].

Questions in order of priority (maximum three): [space for three questions].

The one specific outcome we are trying to achieve from this appointment: [space].

The Intimacy Inventory

Each partner completes this independently, then shares. Not as homework. As a starting point for a specific conversation.

The physical connection I miss most is: [space].

What makes physical closeness feel difficult right now is: [space].

One small thing my partner could do that would help me feel more physically connected is: [space].

One small thing I am willing to try this week is: [space].

The Fertility Conversation Starter

Each partner writes independently. Share only when both feel ready.

My honest hope about the fertility question right now is: [space].

My honest fear about the fertility question right now is: [space].

What I most need from my partner in this conversation is: [space].

What I am afraid of saying out loud is: [space].

The Partner Emotional Audit

Complete privately. Revisit monthly.

The emotional state most prominent for me right now (circle one): guilt / resentment / grief / helplessness / loneliness.

What's driving it, specifically: [space for three sentences].

One concrete step that might reduce it: [space for one sentence].

Date completed: [space]. Date to revisit: [space].

The Support Ecosystem Map

Draw a circle and divide it into four quadrants. Label each quadrant and complete both columns.

Emotional support: what I currently have / what I currently lack.

Practical support: what I currently have / what I currently lack.

Social support: what I currently have / what I currently lack.

Professional support: what I currently have / what I currently lack.

One gap I will address this week: [space]. Specific first step: [space].

References

Bafort, C., Beebeejaun, Y., Tomassetti, C., Bosteels, J., & Duffy, J. M. N. (2020). Laparoscopic surgery for endometriosis. Cochrane Database of Systematic Reviews, 2020(10), CD011031. https://doi.org/10.1002/14651858.CD011031.pub3

Berghmans, B. (2018). Physiotherapy for pelvic pain and female sexual dysfunction: An untapped resource. International Urogynecology Journal, 29(5), 631-638. https://doi.org/10.1007/s00192-017-3536-8

Boivin, J., Griffiths, E., & Venetis, C. A. (2011). Emotional distress in infertile women and failure of assisted reproductive technologies: Meta-analysis of prospective psychosocial studies. BMJ, 342, d223. https://doi.org/10.1136/bmj.d223

Cano, A., Miller, L. R., & Loree, A. (2009). Spouse beliefs about partner chronic pain. The Journal of Pain, 10(5), 486-492. https://doi.org/10.1016/j.jpain.2008.11.005

Culley, L., Law, C., Hudson, N., Denny, E., Mitchell, H., Baumgarten, M., & Raine-Fenning, N. (2013). The social and psychological impact of endometriosis on women's lives: A critical narrative review. Human Reproduction Update, 19(6), 625-639. https://doi.org/10.1093/humupd/dmt027

Culley, L., Law, C., Hudson, N., Mitchell, H., Denny, E., & Raine-Fenning, N. (2017). A qualitative study of the impact of endometriosis on male partners. Human Reproduction, 32(8), 1667-1673. https://doi.org/10.1093/humrep/dex221

el Hadad, S., Schwartz, A. S. K., Gassner, C., Haeberlin, F., von Orelli, S., Imesch, P., & Leeners, B. (2024). Partnership and relationship happiness in endometriosis related chronic pelvic pain: A multicenter case-control study. Frontiers in Psychology, 15, Article 1382067. https://doi.org/10.3389/fpsyg.2024.1382067

Endometriosis UK. (2024). Dismissed, ignored and belittled: The long road to endometriosis diagnosis in the UK. https://www.endometriosis-uk.org/diagnosis-report

European Society of Human Reproduction and Embryology. (2022). ESHRE guideline: Endometriosis. https://www.eshre.eu/Guidelines-and-Legal/Guidelines/Endometriosis-guideline

Figley, C. R. (Ed.). (1995). Compassion fatigue: Coping with secondary traumatic stress disorder in those who treat the traumatized. Brunner/Mazel.

Fryer, J., Mason-Jones, A. J., & Woodward, A. (2025). Understanding diagnostic delay for endometriosis: A scoping review using the social-ecological framework. Health Care for Women International, 46(3), 335-351. https://doi.org/10.1080/07399332.2024.2413056

German IVF Register. (2020). Jahrbuch 2020 [Annual report 2020]. Deutsche IVF-Register e.V. https://www.deutsches-ivf-register.de

Hämmerli, S., Kohl Schwartz, A. S., Geraedts, K., Imesch, P., Rauchfuss, M., Wölfler, M. M., Haeberlin, F., von Orelli, S., Eberhard, M., Imthurn, B., & Leeners, B. (2018). Does endometriosis affect sexual activity and satisfaction of the man partner? A comparison of partners from women diagnosed with endometriosis and controls. The Journal of Sexual Medicine, 15(6), 853-865. https://doi.org/10.1016/j.jsxm.2018.03.087

Jo, J., & Lee, S. H. (2018). Heat therapy for primary dysmenorrhea: A systematic review and meta-analysis of its effects on pain relief and quality of life. Scientific

Reports, 8, Article 16252. https://doi.org/10.1038/s41598-018-34303-z

Martire, L. M., Schulz, R., Helgeson, V. S., Small, B. J., & Saghafi, E. M. (2010). Review and meta-analysis of couple-oriented interventions for chronic illness. Annals of Behavioral Medicine, 40(3), 325-342. https://doi.org/10.1007/s12160-010-9216-2

Matalliotakis, M., Koliarakis, I., Matalliotakis, I., & Bertsias, G. (2021). The social and economic burden of endometriosis. In O. Saridogan & P. Vercellini (Eds.), Current management of endometriosis. IntechOpen.

McGuire, H., Hawton, K., & Pukall, C. F. (2017). Couple-based interventions for sexual dysfunction in women with chronic pelvic pain: A review. Sexual Medicine Reviews, 5(2), 158-167. https://doi.org/10.1016/j.sxmr.2016.11.006

Morotti, M., Vincent, K., & Becker, C. M. (2017). Mechanisms of pain in endometriosis. European Journal of Obstetrics & Gynecology and Reproductive Biology, 209, 8-13. https://doi.org/10.1016/j.ejogrb.2016.07.497

National Institute for Health and Care Excellence. (2024). Endometriosis: Diagnosis and management (NICE guideline NG73). https://www.nice.org.uk/guidance/ng73

Pinquart, M., & Sörensen, S. (2003). Differences between caregivers and noncaregivers in psychological health and physical health: A meta-analysis. Psychology and Aging, 18(2), 250-267. https://doi.org/10.1037/0882-7974.18.2.250

Pukall, C. F., Goldstein, A. T., Bergeron, S., Foster, D., Stein, A., Kellogg-Spadt, S., & Bachmann, G. (2016). Vulvodynia: Definition, prevalence, impact, and pathophysiological factors. The Journal of Sexual Medicine, 13(3), 291-304. https://doi.org/10.1016/j.jsxm.2015.12.021

Santulli, P., Giraudet, G., Estrade, J.-P., Indersie, E., Ravelomanana, M., Collinet, P., Secchi, C., & Arnal, E. (2024). Impact of endometriosis on partners: Results from the French EndoVie survey. European Journal of Obstetrics & Gynecology and Reproductive Biology, 303, 310-316. https://doi.org/10.1016/j.ejogrb.2024.10.040

Tripoli, T. M., Sato, H., Sartori, M. G. F., de Araujo, F. F., Girão, M. J. B. C., & Schor, E. (2011). Evaluation of quality of life and sexual satisfaction in women suffering from chronic pelvic pain with or without endometriosis. The Journal of Sexual Medicine, 8(2), 497-503. https://doi.org/10.1111/j.1743-6109.2010.01976.x

Vercellini, P., Fedele, L., Aimi, G., Pietropaolo, G., Consonni, D., & Crosignani, P. G. (2007). Association between endometriosis stage, lesion type, patient characteristics and severity of pelvic pain symptoms: A multivariate analysis of over 1000 patients. Human Reproduction, 22(1), 266-271. https://doi.org/10.1093/humrep/del339

World Health Organization. (2025, October 15). Endometriosis. https://www.who.int/news-room/fact-sheets/detail/endometriosis

Zarbo, C., Brugnera, A., Frigerio, L., Malandrino, C., Rabboni, M., Bondi, E., & Compare, A. (2018). Psychological and interpersonal profiles in patients with endometriosis: A systematic review. Gynecological Endocrinology, 34(12), 991-1001. https://doi.org/10.1080/09513590.2018.1490407

Zhao, X., Lan, Y., Long, Q., Huang, Y., & Li, Y. (2024). Infertility-related stress, and dyadic coping as predictors of quality of life: Gender differences among couples with infertility issues. BMC Psychology, 12, Article 431. https://doi.org/10.1186/s40359-024-01912-5

Zondervan, K. T., Becker, C. M., & Missmer, S. A. (2020). Endometriosis. New England Journal of Medicine, 382(13), 1244-1256. https://doi.org/10.1056/NEJMra1810764

Zurlo, M. C., Cattaneo Della Volta, M. F., & Vallone, F. (2020). Infertility-related stress and psychological health outcomes in infertile couples undergoing medical treatments: Testing a multi-dimensional model. Journal of Clinical Psychology in Medical Settings, 27(4), 662-676. https://doi.org/10.1007/s10880-019-09653-z

www.ingramcontent.com/pod-product-compliance
Lightning Source LLC
LaVergne TN
LVHW050303210926
848481LV00014BA/809
* 9 7 8 1 7 6 4 7 2 6 5 5 9 *